FROM THE HOMEFRONT

MEMOIRS OF A MILITARY SPOUSE

SANDY HOPE STEWART

LUCIDBOOKS

**To God,
my Life, my Hope**

**To Bill,
my Sailor, my Love**

From the Homefront:
Memoirs of a Military Spouse

Copyright © 2023 by Sandy Hope Stewart

Published by Lucid Books in Houston, TX
www.LucidBooks.com

ISBN: 978-1-63296-612-4
eISBN: 978-1-63296-613-1

Special Sales: Most Lucid Books titles are available in special quantity discounts. Custom imprinting or excerpting can also be done to fit special needs. Contact Lucid Books at Info@LucidBooks.com

"In a world where the valor and sacrifices of our military members often take center stage, there is a remarkable and untold story that unfolds behind the scenes—the unwavering strength and resilience of military spouses. Infused with hard-won wisdom, Sandy Stewart's transparent story is an invitation to embrace life as it comes, find lessons in the unknown, and depend on God above all else. In *From the Home Front: Memoirs of a Military Spouse,* Sandy takes us on a powerful journey, offering an intimate glimpse into the hearts and souls of those left behind.

This memoir is a poignant tribute to God who faithfully showed up extraordinarily in the ordinary. Her lively anecdotes illustrate how He walked with her in her effort to hold the fort, provide unwavering support, and face countless challenges with grace. With raw honesty and profound vulnerability, she invites us into her world, unveiling the intricacies of her daily struggles, her fears, and her determination to stay connected— to her sailor, herself, and her Savior".

—Dr. Kristie Polk
Psychology Professor

"In this book Sandy Stewart takes readers behind the scenes and into the home of a military family by honestly opening up her heart and sharing her struggles and joys of supporting her husband. This book is a wonderful short read that left me more grateful to God for all of the people who serve our country and the families that support them!"

—Aaron Anderson,
Sr. Pastor, Sovereign Grace Church,
Woodstock, GA

Contents

Introduction

Have you ever considered what you would do if your spouse called you in the middle of the day and blurted out that he was leaving the next morning and didn't know where he was going or when he would be back?

Neither had I! It was early November 1979. Our boys were five and three years old, and our baby girl was two. We had been a military family for less than three years and had been living in military base housing for a year. There were no immediate deployment plans for my husband's squadron, so our life looked like that of most young families. He was working long hours, but he was home every night and on weekends.

The Thanksgiving holiday was approaching, and we were excited to be going home for the holiday. On the day of the call, I was busy packing for a short family getaway. A getaway, it turns out, that would not happen because serving in the military is a family affair, and sacrifices are made by all.

Mine is the story of one such military spouse's experiences and one such military family's sacrifices during a difficult time in our nation's history.

Each military member and each military family member have different experiences and different takes on the ones they share.

This memoir is two-fold in that it speaks to the many challenges I faced as a military spouse and how God used it all to reveal how broken I was and how faithful He is to put the pieces back together.

My memoir is not, by any means, to be compared to the level of sacrifice made by so many of our military brothers and sisters. The military members who have given the ultimate sacrifice and their families' losses, as well as those who have suffered physical, emotional, or psychological injuries, are, by far, worthy of much more appreciation and honor than anything our family has experienced.*

I hope you will enjoy my memoir as I invite you along on the journey from the past to the present of this very ordinary woman who believes that we all live extraordinary lives.

We all have a story to tell. I hope that some of you will read mine and be encouraged to tell your extraordinary life story as well.

---

* A portion of the proceeds from this book goes toward the support of non-profit military and first responders organizations.

Chapter 1

Living and Loving Retirement

I'm relaxing on our chaise, enjoying the view from our sliding glass door that leads onto a balcony overlooking the community club and swimming pool. The small set of chimes dings softly as I watch the birds on the roof of the building across the way. They seem to be playing a game of catch-me-if-you-can. One flies at the other and takes off. The other pursues him, and they do a funny little dance. The scene repeats itself several times before they fly out of sight.

I hear distant traffic and the sound of a very distant train. It's not really a train but rather the sound our refrigerator makes from time to time. I love the sound of trains, and I welcome it. Trains always remind me of my dad. He was a railroad man his entire adult life.

My husband of 50 years and I moved here a few months ago, but we are still not finished unpacking all the boxes. There is a good reason for that. Between coming and going shortly after moving in and having ankle replacement surgery shortly after returning, we were tired. I was in a good bit of pain leading up to and following the surgery.

The week that we moved in, our son remarried. The following weekend, our granddaughter married out of town.

We flew from there to Amsterdam to board a cruise ship to Ireland and Iceland. We are blessed to cruise often with our dear friends of 46 years. We were home a short time before heading to Canada, where our daughter lives with her husband, two of our nine grandchildren, and one of our four fur grand-babies. We are blessed to visit our kids and grands several times each year. Our oldest lives in our area with his sweet wife, three kids, two cute doggies, and a sweet kitty. We see them every few days.

Our second son lives in the Atlanta area with his wonderful wife, three of their four children, and a sweet doggy. The oldest, recently married, lives close by them. We are incredibly blessed to visit them often as well.

As is the norm, traveling south also included a visit with my husband's sister and her husband. We have lived a lot of life together. We have shared great laughs and weathered many storms side by side. There are storms in our paths even now. To be best friends with those who are also family is a very special blessing.

They were my lifeline during the most difficult time of my life. We were connected then, and we are still connected today. Our stays there almost always include a visit or two with my best friend from high school. She is more like a sister than a friend.

Alas, fully settling in will be accomplished, but our priority will always be friends and family. When you have lived a long while and endured many trials, one cannot help but appreciate the quiet, stress-free days. Life does not always afford us such.

Chapter 2

It's a Calling

My husband and I met, were engaged, and then married within two months time in 1972.

We met on a blind date set up by his sister, with whom I worked. He had just turned 23, and I was 20. I suppose you could say that our date went well since we saw each other the next two nights, and on that third date, he asked me to marry him! As if that's not crazy enough, with no hesitation, I actually said yes!

Just shy of our first anniversary, I went forward at a Billy Graham Crusade in our hometown and asked Jesus into my heart and into my life. About one week later, my husband did the same in the living room of our small one-bedroom apartment. More about that later.

Our first baby was born in September 1974 and our second in July 1976. In the summer of 1976, my husband was working at a paper company, and I was staying home with our boys. The youngest was only a few months old when my husband began talking about missing his helicopter days (he had been in the Army and had been home from Viet Nam a couple of years before we met).

With my blessing, he decided to join the local Army National Guard, although the thought of him flying didn't thrill me. But his doing so gave him the opportunity to return to his first love and brought in much-needed extra income for our little family.

Within a few months and after talking to his brother, who was in the Navy, he came to me about his desire to join the Navy.

Wait a minute . . . what in the world are you talking about?

He was saying, "I'm thinking about joining the Navy and applying for brother duty."

But I was hearing, "I really want to leave you and the boys, jump on a ship, and travel the world for months at a time."

Why, oh why would you want to do that?

I had never considered military life and was not interested in doing so then. Just thinking about it was frightening. I'm sure he thought he was offering me a bit of comfort by telling me that he was hoping to get into a helicopter squadron and not join a ship's crew.

More helicopters?

More flying?

Don't they crash all the time?

Eventually, as I came to understand his strong desire to serve our country, I prayed, turned it over to God's control, and truly supported him. I have come to recognize that the military, much like ministry and first responders, is often more than a profession or job: it is a calling.

And so, out of my comfort zone I stepped, and into the role of a military spouse I leaped, albeit with much fear and trepidation.

Chapter 3

First Came the Leap
into Faith

For several months before I met my husband, I had been
living each day to its fullest and waiting. I had no idea
exactly what I was waiting for. I was searching but had
no idea what I was searching for or that I was searching at all.

I know now that the restlessness I was experiencing was
indeed my search for love. I had recently ended a 2-and-a-half-
year relationship with my high school boyfriend. I was bored.
I was confused. I was also headed, at a rapid pace, down a path
of self-destruction.

I was dating several people and looking for love in all the
wrong places. I was becoming arrogant and cynical. I developed
a foul mouth. I did not like that side of me, but it reared its
ugly head anyway.

I met my husband in August 1972. I was working in a small
branch office of the World Book Encyclopedia in Raleigh, NC.

My family moved to Raleigh from Baltimore in December 1961 when I was 9 1/2 years old. I loved Raleigh as much as a 20-year-old can love where they live. But I was contemplating moving to Tampa, FL, where my best friend from high school had moved a few months prior.

If I had actually done so, this memoir would tell a completely different story. The what-ifs in life can be mere contemplations, or they can be the cause of much regret. Thankfully, for me, it is the former.

As I shared earlier, I went forward at a Billy Graham crusade and received Jesus into my heart. Leading up to my decision on September 28, 1973, was, I believe, the absolute work of God in my life before I even asked Him. After meeting my Savior that night, I knew that He was what I was waiting for. God knew that He was Whom I was searching for.

Exactly what happened leading up to and immediately following my conversion is quite remarkable, especially considering that we went from our marriage ending, my husband having no interest in saving our marriage, and neither of us interested in being spiritually saved—to my salvation, his salvation, and the restoration of our marriage all in about one week!

It played out like this: about a month shy of our one-year anniversary, I noticed a change in him. Something was not the same, so I asked him what was going on. What was going on sent me into a tailspin! He was not sure if he wanted to remain married. Not being one to turn to God, I set about to fix everything. I said all the right things; I was loving and understanding and willing to make changes. Surely, he would see the light. But he did not see the light, and the darkness around us was seemingly impenetrable.

I was not ready to give up the fight, so I took drastic measures. I decided to go to his mother and tell her what her son was doing. Surely, she would set him straight. I did know that she and most of his family were, what I considered at that time, religious, but I was not at all prepared for how she handled the news about her wayward son. We went to her bedroom. She sat on the side of the bed, and I sat in a rocking chair in front of her. She took me through the Bible from Genesis to Revelation. I thought she would never finish her discourse.

Oh, my goodness, I get it! All the answers to the problems in the world are found in the Bible. Blah, Blah, Blah! NOW, what are you going to do about your son?

Don't get me wrong, I really did love my mother-in-law very much. She passed at the age of 92 in 2019, and I miss her dearly. We would say that she was Naomi to my Ruth. Her God became my God, and her people became my people. That did not, however, happen on that day.

On that day, all I could see was that she obviously did not understand my situation. I left there deflated and defeated. What I didn't consciously realize was that I also left there with words of hope.

She would ask me a couple of days later to attend the Billy Graham Crusade; the rest is history. Or should I say HIS story! Just a few nights after my conversion, I was sitting on the side of our bed as my husband was telling me he was leaving. I was sobbing.

As he turned to leave the room, he looked over at me and said, "Just don't lose what you have!"

When he was out of my sight, with his hand on the doorknob to leave, I yelled at him through uncontrollable sobs, "If it's so good, why don't you want it?"

He removed his hand, turned, walked to the kitchen phone, dialed his parents' home phone, and sobbed into the phone that he needed help.

It was around midnight. His parents happened to be hosting some men who were in town from Europe to teach. They all got up and came straight to our place, where my husband received the gift of salvation. On October 21, 1973, we would celebrate our first anniversary by deciding to start a family. I could not have imagined then that the life of a military spouse awaited me, but I did know that God most certainly had a plan for us.

Chapter 4

When God Reveals Himself Supernaturally

God first revealed Himself to me in a very personal way the night that I went forward to receive Jesus as my Savior. I was extremely self-conscious, and standing up in front of a stadium full of strangers was something that I would have avoided like the plague.

But with my heart pounding and some unseen force pulling me out of my seat, I stood and made my way to the field. As I made my way down the many bleachers, everywhere I looked, I saw black circles instead of faces. If folks were looking at me, and I'm sure some were, I did not know it.

It was a small thing, but it did not go unnoticed by me. I knew that I was encountering someone who knew me intimately and loved me still.

The second time I experienced such power happened soon

after we were saved. I was in the bathroom of our apartment, getting ready for work. I lit a cigarette (almost everyone smoked in their homes then), inhaled deeply, and before I even had a chance to exhale, I heard a loud voice. I cannot say that it was audible. Neither can I say that it was not.

"You don't need those anymore!"

I knew it was God, and I could not put that cigarette out quickly enough. I had smoked for only three years, but I was smoking two packs a day. After taking two more puffs later that day, I would never touch another cigarette.

My husband decided to quit with me. He had been smoking since he was a young teen. We each had a carton of cigarettes in the home, and we never smoked another one.

The third such encounter occurred shortly thereafter. We were visiting his brother and sister-in-law for a long weekend. They lived in a small trailer with their two little girls. Since there was no extra bedroom, we slept on a mat by the door in the living area.

Before calling it a night, we had been talking about God and His Son, Jesus. My brother-in-law was saying that he would not be able to look at Jesus if he came face to face with Him. I didn't say anything, but I thought how I would be just the opposite.

If I saw Jesus in person, I would race to Him and embrace Him.

I was a bit wound up and having trouble falling asleep. After laying there for a while, I heard something that I can only describe as the 'swooshing of robes.'

I froze! I buried my head in my pillow! I held my breath! And I most certainly did not stand to embrace Him. And I kept the whole thing to myself. I was sure that I must have imagined it. At the same time, I knew that I had not.

I told my husband about it just a few years ago. Instead of saying it was probably my imagination, which I expected, he told me that he, too, had heard it, which I had not expected!

Why these three events took place within a short period of time very early in my conversion, I do not know. It is a mystery to me. As is the possibility that God will reveal Himself supernaturally to me ever again. The fact that He did so three times greatly humbles me.

Chapter 5

Before the Leaps

On June 28, 1952, the third child was born to a couple in Baltimore, MD. She weighed exactly 7 pounds, about 2 pounds heavier than any of her four siblings' birth weights. Soon after returning home, it became clear to her parents that she was unable to digest the baby formula.

After every available brand of baby formula was offered and proven intolerable, the parents were instructed to take her to Johns Hopkins Hospital. Their baby was failing to thrive and needed emergency care. Hospitalization, tests, attempted feedings, as well as a panel of pediatricians working together to find an answer, did nothing to change the situation.

After determining that there was nothing to be done, the doctors told the parents, "Take her home and pray."

The 25-year-old father, not being a praying man, instead decided to try something rather unorthodox in infant feeding. He stopped at a grocery store on the way home and bought a gallon of whole milk. They began feeding it to their baby, and she began to thrive. And still is. That baby girl was me. I do wonder if my battle with intestinal issues over the years may have something to do with having whole milk as an infant. It is only a curiosity, as I am thankful that my dad thought to do so. I consider him my hero. He was one of the smartest people I have ever known, and it amazes me that he was thinking so far outside the box.

He died in 1982 at the age of 54 from cancer. I was 29 when he passed. How I would love to have known him longer and better. I have also wondered why my mother did not choose breastfeeding, but it was never mentioned in the retelling of the story. To my knowledge, she did not breastfeed any of her five children.

This and many questions went unasked and unanswered because I never took the time to ask. She lived to be 91 years old, and I still did not have enough time with her. I miss them both very much.

Chapter 6

The Leap into Military Life

We had to jump through several hoops to make it possible for my husband to return to the military. Financially, we had to prove that we could afford to live at his starting pay grade. To do so, we had to sell our fairly new Ford Pinto Wagon. I really loved that car. We bought an 8-year-old Chevrolet Impala. I really disliked that car.

He had to get several character references, and we moved out of our apartment. Once all the requirements were checked off, he left for a month-long indoctrination into the Navy. The boys and I stayed with his parents in the interim.

We slept in basement bedrooms. At that time, parents were warned against sleeping with their children, and frankly, it was not something that even entered my mind. As I look back, I realize that it would have been a very good idea for us to have done so in the unheated basement during the coldest winter month.

We survived our month of basement-dwelling, reunited with our new military man, and headed to a place that was further away than I had ever been from home. We did not qualify for a military-provided move, so off we went in a rental moving van. After loading our littles and our few belongings, we shared tearful goodbyes with family and friends, and began our long trek toward military life.

My thoughts were swirling.

What is this new life going to look like?

What are the rules I need to know?

Aren't there lots of rules?

Can I even drive on the base?

Where are we going to live?

We had made arrangements to stay with friends of my brother-in-law, but I didn't know them, and I was insecure and nervous around people I didn't know, and we would be staying with them until we found a place to live.

What if they really don't want us there?

What if we can't find anything we can afford?

What if I end up being the worst military spouse the Navy has ever known?

My imagination fed off my anxiety. All the mental anxiety (a condition I do not remember hearing about in those days) had a powerfully negative effect on my physical health. By the time we stopped at a motel (we certainly could not afford a hotel) overnight, I was suffering from a terrible sinus condition that kept me pacing the whole night. At least my military man and my babies slept beautifully. One scripture that I memorized soon after being saved was when Jesus gives the invitation:

> "Come to me, all you who are weary and burdened, and I will give you rest. Take my yoke upon you and learn from me, for I am gentle and humble in heart, and you will find rest for your souls. For my yoke is easy and my burden is light." *(Matt. 11:28-30)*

Like most scripture, it was in my head, but I would endure much more weariness and carry many more burdens before I would begin to know it in my heart and live by its promise. God faithfully uses all of life's challenges to bring us to that place of rest and peace.

The family we stayed with was lovely. They graciously opened their home to us and welcomed us like old friends. The very next day, we began our search for a place to live. We found a nice 3-bedroom apartment just a few miles from the base and moved in within a week. We began attending our new friends' church, and things were falling into place. It took several weeks to get well from the sinus infection and chest discomfort brought on by stress. I did not understand then the part that stress and anxiety had played in my lifelong battles with migraines, lung infections, and serious intestinal issues. It was a pattern that would continue to play out time and again.

Chapter 7

Out of My Comfort Zone

Even though I had always been socially active in school, I was not exactly outgoing. I certainly was not one to introduce myself to a complete stranger, but I guess I took stepping out of my comfort zone seriously and did just that.

I knew that the couple across the hall from us had two little girls just about the ages as our boys. One morning while my boys were napping, I poured two cups of coffee (which was very expensive at the time), stepped across the hall, took a deep breath, and knocked on her door. As she opened the door, I simply asked if she liked coffee. She did and immediately embraced my gesture. We became friends for life that day.

She invited us over for dessert that night, and before the evening ended, we were on the floor working on our post-pregnancy tummy flattening with a wheel exerciser. While looking through some photos, I asked her how far along she was in one of them. Instead of showing us to the door, she laughed and said she had already had the baby. That's when I knew for sure that she was my kind of person. I did, however, make a mental note never to do that again! Our husbands talked about the military all night, and the beginning of a beautiful friendship had begun. As it would turn out, we would all be going to the same area once the guys' schooling was finished.

Maybe this whole military thing really will work out okay.

And perhaps the days of being overly shy would be behind me now.

Chapter 8

Socially Active/ Socially Awkward

While working in the counselor's office in high school, I decided to look at my file. Everything was paper then, and it was easy enough to find my name in the alphabetized folders.

My first-grade teacher had written that I was "painfully shy."

I don't think I read any further. Her evaluation was a bit of a shock to me. I knew this about myself, but I had no idea that it was so obvious to others. As I had done with such encounters as far back as I can remember, I made a conscious decision to somehow cover up this weakness, this insecurity.

Because I was a cheerleader from grades 8-12, I was considered part of the popular crowd. It is at least assumed that you are popular, and in many ways, you are, but popularity can be a two-edged sword. I was part of the in-crowd, most of whom were wealthier, prettier, more confident, and more self-assured than me. At least, that was my perception. The wealthier part was definitely a factor. Our high school was a county school. Kids who lived within city limits all went to the city school in close proximity to their homes. It was common knowledge that those 'city school kids' looked down on us 'county school kids' as if we were all poor, unintelligent, and lacking in sophistication.

The truth is, we had amazing diversity in our school. We came from everywhere in the county outside the city limits. I went to school with kids who lived close by and others who lived as far as 15 miles or more away from me. There were kids with superior intellect. I was not one of them, but I was friends with my share of them. There were kids from wealthy families, kids from poor families, and most, like me, from somewhere in between.

All of this played into the two-edged sword of being popular, and thus being noticed. Being noticed was not something I enjoyed except when I was in my cheerleading uniform. Then I was proud to be noticed. I was relaxed. My uniform hid my shy and awkward tendencies. I loved the role. I was in my element in front of the crowd. I suppose a bit like Spider-Man or Super Man, my uniform emboldened me. I truly loved my school, our sports, and our teams. I understood sports: the rules, the regulations, and the roles of the players.

Almost all my self-consciousness was due to the focus on clothes, shoes, and purses during those high school years. While most kids I associated with would wear a different outfit for three weeks in a row, there were times when I had to wear the same clothes two or three times in the same week.

This was terribly humiliating for me. I did the only thing I knew to do to not bring attention to this. I would wear my coat all day except for the one or two days a week when we wore our cheerleading uniforms. I can only imagine that my attempt to keep attention away actually did just the opposite.

I am sure that it was obvious that the only time I wasn't 'cold' was when I was in my beloved blue and white uniform. At the same time that I was terribly self-conscious, I also dated and had boyfriends throughout my high school years. I look back now and realize that most of us are multifaceted, and those teenage years produce many sides to our personalities.

When one of the wealthiest girls in our circle invited several of us over to try on shoes she no longer wanted, I was thrilled. She always had the cutest shoes. Papagallos brand shoes were to die for, and I owned exactly zero pairs. She probably owned every style and color available. I coveted those shoes. I left there so sad and mad that my feet, compared to hers, were like those of Anastasia and Drizella.

The first thing I did when I started working after graduation was to buy a new wardrobe in all the latest fashions, complete with Papagallos and purses to match. My days of dressing like those I so envied would continue for about three years.

Even after realizing that others are not paying near as much attention to me as I thought, I would continue to fall back into the trap of self-mindedness for years to come.

Chapter 9

Childhood Besties

The truth is, though, I have wonderful memories of those high school years. I had two close friends. One lived about a mile from me, and one lived about eight or more miles from me. My friend who lived close by would come to pick me up on her dad's motorcycle. I would climb on the back, and off we'd go back to her house. I think we did wear helmets, but we most certainly did not wear any protective clothing.

I do not remember my parents ever speaking of any concerns. I'm not sure they even knew. Helicopter parenting was non-existent. Of course, we now realize all the dangers we encountered, but at the time, we were living enchanted lives.

My best friend and I met in 9th grade in home economics class. I thought she was the funniest person ever. We found out later that we had actually played together when all of our parents were in a bowling league. Neither of us remembered it.

She and I would spend all four high school years practically joined at the hip. I might have spent more nights at her house than my own. Well, maybe it was a close second. Her dad was a gruff man who was a teddy bear deep down inside. But I never met his deep down inside personality, and I was quite afraid of him. I should say I was afraid of his deep, angry-sounding voice.

On the other hand, my friend and my dad were like buddies, always bantering back and forth. They were equally witty and would keep at it until I found a reason for us to move on. I was never quite as witty as either of them.

I always loved staying at her house. I lived in the country on a one-lane road with five houses on it; it was pretty isolated. She lived in a great neighborhood with tons of our friends. We risked life and limb to spend as much time as we could socializing.

Since I was scared of her dad and she knew better than to cross him, we were forced to devise a plan to sneak out that guaranteed our success. She would unlock the basement door ahead of time, and when we knew her parents were asleep, we jumped out of her bedroom window, which was about four feet off the ground, rolling down the hill as soon as we landed. We would take off running, holding back our laughter until we were a good distance away. We would roam the neighborhood all night, often meeting up with other kids.

Sometimes we would climb over the fence to the pool and swim in our clothes—no skinny dipping for us. Just before dawn, we would return through the unlocked basement door and gingerly make our way up the stairs. Because the stairs creaked very loudly and her dad was a very loud snorer, we would take a step each time he snored and quickly stop to wait for the next snore. We were successful every single time. It was one of many ways we lived life on the edge.

Once in the heat and humidity of summer, we walked the eight miles from my house to hers. I have no idea how many hours it took us, up and down hills, over railroad tracks, and turning down offers of rides (even then, we were told not to ride with strangers). We could not wait to get to her house, put on our bathing suits, and head to the pool. Imagine my utter dismay when, just as we reached the top of a hill with her house in sight, we also sighted my older brother sitting in our Volkswagen Bus, fuming. He had been waiting way too long, and he was adamant that I get in and get in fast. He made it clear that he would not be back to get me. And so, off we went. All I could do was look longingly at the pool as we drove past it. My brother, who was almost always caring and understanding, was not moved in the least by my crying all the way home. I'm sure he was dealing with his own teenage issues.

My fellow escapee and I have remained close all these years. Even when military life took me far away, we remained in touch. We still see each other often and speak almost every week. I dearly cherish our 56-year friendship.

Chapter 10

Military Life
(the First Few Months)

I am not sure that I had even been to a zoo before moving to our first military assignment, but even with our very tight budget, we managed to pull together enough money for a couple of annual zoo passes. The kids were free. It was our outlet, our family time, our entertainment, and we loved it. We would later take the kids to our local zoo once we moved to our new duty station, but we would not come close to the number of visits those few months.

I think the animals there even recognized us!

When we weren't visiting the zoo, we were attending church activities, going to parks, and enjoying picnics. One day, along with our friends from across the hall, we drove across the state line just to say we had been to that state. We had a picnic lunch at the State Line Welcome Center and turned right back around, and came home. We could then add that one to the names of states that we'd been to, even if only for a couple of hours.

Spur-of-the-moment activities were new to me. I loved it! I started learning to sew because my friend was an excellent seamstress and was so kind to teach me. I was a bit of a slow learner, but she was very patient and a great teacher. We spent many days sewing or handcrafting.

I was truly enjoying this new life, and time was moving along quickly. Near the end of our time there, something happened to my husband that would be a key element in a much bigger moment just a few years later.

He had joined the church softball team and had come home late one night, unable to walk. He had injured his ankle and needed to go to the Naval Hospital ER. Our friend across the hall was still awake, studying. He kindly offered to take my husband to the ER.

The ankle injury was quite severe, requiring about six months in a cast and subsequent surgeries. He began riding into work each morning with the fellow who would become his best friend and mentor. It all started with a cup of coffee.

My baby boy was about six months old when something happened in me that I had never experienced before. I was changing his diaper, talking to him, and loving on him when he smiled at me. Of course, that was not the first time he had smiled at me, but there was something in this smile. It brought tears to my eyes. I felt that a part of my heart had been touched that had never been touched before. I fell head-over-heels in love with him. What happened in my heart next is a bit of a mystery even to this day, except to say that I know it was from the Lord. I had an overwhelming desire to have another baby. I really thought my husband would think I was crazy, but he said OK! The next month #3 was on the way.

Oh my, what was I thinking?

How am I going to do this?

As soon as my friend found out, she decided she wanted another one too. A month later, #3 was on the way for them too. We would all do this together. It would be one of the many things we did together.

Chapter 11

You're On Your Own Now, Girl

I was 8 months pregnant with our third, and our boys were 3 and 15 months when my husband's schooling ended. Since he now qualified for a military-provided move, the four of us made our way back those 750 miles. I came to appreciate that Impala for its reliability, if nothing else.

We would stay at his folks' house for a few days and then head the 200 miles to our new duty station. Our good friends were already there, and my husband's sister and her husband, who was from that area, were there too. We had a long drive ahead of us, as well as setting up our household in the home we would be renting.

We had decided that because of our ongoing tight budget, if the boys handled the trip well, we would not stop overnight anywhere. We would stop for food, gas, diaper changes, and bathroom needs, but that was it. We were excited to be going to our new home. Not once did he or I think about, nor did any doctor mention, that it was not wise to travel so far with so few stops at 8 months pregnant. Our parents didn't even address any concerns.

I think we just did what we had to do and made the best of it. Because we now live in a time of voicing concerns much more readily, and even more so because of my own experience, I would advise my daughters to take much more time with many more stops and at least one overnight stop. But it was a different time, and not a thought was given to any consequences to my baby or me.

As it turned out, the boys slept almost the whole way, and we did exactly as planned. We drove straight through, stopping rarely. By the time we reached his parent's home, I was beyond exhausted. Of course, I had been pretty tired throughout this pregnancy, having been pregnant for the third time in three years and keeping up with two toddlers.

But this was a whole different level of exhaustion than I had ever experienced. I have no memory whatsoever of making the trip to our rental home, setting up our household, or much of anything after the long drive until a few days before our baby was born. I do remember going out to the picnic table in the backyard to write a short letter. Yes, we wrote letters then. Lots of letters filled with old news but cherished all the same. Besides the home phone, it was how we communicated, and I enjoyed using this method of communication often. I still do.

I sat down with paper and pen in hand and simply did not

have the energy to write a single word. I'm not sure how close to my due date this was, but my husband had already left for a school across the country. The news that he was required to attend this school and that not doing so would be detrimental to his career hit very hard.

According to his orders, he would return home two days before the baby's due date.

Wow! This military life is nothing to take lightly.

I was learning in the school of hard knocks that there was very little I had any control over. But I knew the God who did, and once again, I was turning it over to Him. At least, I thought I was. It is always the absolute best thing we can do, but there are times, especially in our early walk with Him, that it surely is not easy, and it surely does not feel that He is in control. This was most definitely one of those times.

I had an appointment four days before the baby's due date to be seen at the Naval Clinic in the area for the first time. I expected to go in, get weighed, have a chat with the doctor, and leave, only to head to the Naval Hospital with my husband once in labor.

But when I mentioned to the doctor that I was experiencing something that I had not in my other two pregnancies, he decided to do a thorough examination which indicated that some of the amniotic fluid was leaking.

This news was followed by him telling me to go home, pack my things, and return to the hospital that afternoon to have labor induced! I was in shock! I desperately asked that we wait a few days until my husband returned home. I was getting ready to beg him to reconsider when he explained that the risk of infection to my baby and me was too great to wait.

Ok, I can do this! I have to do this!

I don't know if I can do this!

Once in my car, I did what I had been doing a lot of . . . I prayed and cried. And cried and prayed. And prayed some more! I prayed that my labor would start on its own. I had never had my labor induced and planned to give birth to this baby completely naturally, as I had with my now 16-month-old baby.

I had a very frightening experience with pain medication with my first baby's birth and had determined that I would never do that again. It so rattled me that, even though I never felt the first labor pain with him, I chose to feel every single one over feeling none, so as not to be left terribly vulnerable and completely dependent on the care of others.

I was really scared! I had never had a baby without my husband there with me. I had also never had a baby in a military hospital.

My dear sister-in-law was at my house caring for her little girl and my boys while I went to my appointment. As soon as I got home and explained everything to her, she managed to contact her husband. He rushed over to watch the children so that she could come with me to the hospital. Thankfully, the hospital had approved of her being with me through labor and delivery.

I wasn't able to contact my husband. I had no phone number and no idea what school, much less which class he was in. And so, just like that, I kissed my little guys goodbye and left to have a baby. I was feeling some labor pangs.

Without any conscious thought, I was in the driver's seat, and we were headed to a place I had never been. It hadn't crossed my mind to find out where it was because my husband was supposed to be driving and knew exactly how to get there.

I had a vague idea of which highway to take, and I remembered hearing that a tunnel was involved. Still, here we were, two young women, neither of whom knew the area very well, hoping we were heading in the right direction. One of us was also experiencing some pretty strong contractions, and she was the driver!

With panic rising, I decided to stop at a gas station and get some directions. I sat in the car trying to ignore but also thanking God for the labor pains that were continuing.

I know now why I didn't switch places with my sister-in-law right then and there. I did not process this at the time, but I now know that I instinctively did what I believed I had to do to maintain some semblance of control in a situation that felt very much out of control.

With exact directions, we made it to the hospital without further delays. We arrived at the hospital around 2:00 in the afternoon, and I was immediately set up in a room with my sister-in-law by my side. It had been decided by the powers that be that I would receive a Pitocin drip to "get my labor started and keep it going quickly."

There was a very sweet young intern assigned to be with me to monitor my labor progress. I told her that my labor was well underway and that I absolutely did not want any meds to speed it up. She agreed to honor my wishes but would keep monitoring me. The intern had been watching me more closely than I realized because, after about 2 1/2 hours, she told me I was in transition, the final stage of labor before the birth.

I had no idea that my labor had progressed to the last stage so quickly. Compared to my last birth, it was not nearly as intense as I expected. Although I wasn't sure she was correct, I soon became aware that my baby was moving through the birth canal.

I knew it! I knew what it felt like, and I was feeling it! I asked my sister-in-law to please get the nurse to check on me. The nurse took her time coming, and when she did, she stood in the doorway and explained to me in a rather condescending tone that it was too soon for me to be checked.

I like to think that birthing mothers are taken a bit more seriously these days, but I was not on that day 46 years ago. I was beginning to panic, and after just a couple more minutes, I again asked my sister-in-law to get the nurse. This time the nurse entered the room, rolled her eyes and begrudgingly checked my progress. "Get her to the delivery room! STAT!"

Well, I certainly tried to tell you!

No apology was offered. None was necessary; the goal was accomplished.

Before I knew it, my baby was in the arms of the doctor. Then he and my baby were gone! Not a single word was spoken. He and several other doctors and nurses were standing around a small table that I knew held my baby, although not visible to me.

Hmm, I guess they do things differently in the Navy.

With absolutely no panic, I asked my sister-in-law, who was standing behind my head, if she could tell if it was a boy or a girl. She couldn't see from where she stood.

It sure is taking them a long time!

Still, there was no concern on my part. I continued to assume it was different in military hospitals. It was quite sometime before the doctor, his glasses covered in blood, came back to me, holding my little one and apologizing for taking off with her that way.

The cord had been very tight around her neck, and they had no time to waste in getting it off. I was allowed to see her briefly, but I could not hold her because they wanted to check her out right away.

Okay, now I'm freaking out!

Also, that doctor is my hero!

I had never met him before her birth. He was simply the doctor on duty. I never saw him again, but I will never forget him. The birth certificate would record the time of birth as 5:31 p.m., roughly three and a half hours after checking in.

I wonder if I did something wrong that caused the cord to be so tight around her neck.

I wonder if that long and exhausting drive had something to do with it.

I silently questioned my poor judgment.

Many years later, I would relay this story to a labor and

delivery nurse practitioner, and she told me that he was MY doctor. For him to leave me, his patient, to save the baby says that it was a very serious, life-or-death situation. Such a sobering thought!

Because my husband and I had agreed that this would be our last child, I was scheduled to have a tubal ligation the next morning. I was not able to see my baby on the day of her birth because she was being carefully monitored.

The first thing the next morning, I was wheeled into the operating room for surgery. That part is very surreal to me. I had been through so much emotionally and physically that I felt like a shadow of myself and incredibly sad to have had no time to bond with my newborn daughter. I was scared and desperately needed to speak to my husband, which was obviously not going to happen.

Adding to my anxiety was the fact that I was awake during the procedure. The operating room felt like a freezer. My arms were laid open and strapped down. The table was tilted back, and I thought for sure I was going to slide right off. I don't remember anyone speaking to me, much less offering any words of comfort.

I so needed my husband with me. It would be a few more days before that happened, but I did finally speak to him that afternoon.

The maternity section of the Naval Hospital was in the old hospital that was built before the Civil War. There were no phones in the rooms, so when a call came in for me at the nurse's station, I was wheeled up.

I was so weak that my voice was a whisper. We managed a very short conversation that I do not remember other than him telling me that he had received a notice from the Red Cross that his baby daughter had been born. A few minutes later, as he entered the classroom, his instructor gave him an enthusiastic congratulations on the birth of his son! He appreciated being able to clarify now that he did indeed have a daughter.

I just wanted him to come home. I would deal with resentment toward him for many years. I was 25 years old at the time with much to learn about the damage that is done by harboring such feelings. He was 28 with much to learn about comforting a physically, mentally, and emotionally scarred wife.

Chapter 12

I Can't Pay for
My Baby!

y baby and I were released from the hospital the
following evening. I don't know what other
hospitals' policies were or if it is still the case at
military hospitals today, but at that time, a patient could be
released any time of day or night.

On this particular occasion, it was close to 8:00 p.m. before
discharge papers had been signed. There was one item to
be taken care of, and then we were good to go. One of the
great benefits of serving in the military is free healthcare.
Although there was no charge for the birth, the baby's care, the
surgery, or my care, there was a small charge of $4.00 a day for
my food.

I owed $16 for the four days. I had somehow handled the
stress and anxiety, the fear, the loneliness, the roller-coaster of
emotions, the physical exhaustion, and considerable pain with

a stoic performance. That is exactly what it was, a performance. But this, this was the final straw.

The $16 might as well have been $16,000. I had no money. I was embarrassed that I could not afford my baby. My pride was destroyed. My last bit of strength was sucked out of me.

I could not turn to my husband.

What are they going to do with my baby and me?

I don't know what to do or say or think!

I was assured it was okay, and that we could still leave the hospital. The $16 would be deducted from my husband's pay over several pay periods. Over several pay periods! That speaks volumes about the low pay at the time. But it also speaks to the willingness of the military to allow it to be done over time, even if it was just $16.

We would face many financial difficulties over the years. My husband worked very hard throughout his career and made advancements along the way. There would be many more separations and sacrifices over the years. When advancement to a higher rank was particularly hard to reach, he would persevere and try again and again.

He would go on to be selected for the warrant officer program and would retire from the Navy as a chief warrant officer. Because of his dedication to his country and his retirement rank, we are blessed to have a comfortable retirement.

But I will never, as long I live, forget when I did not have $16 to pay for our baby!

Chapter 13

A Three-Year-Old, a Sixteen-Month Old, and a Newborn

It must have been well past 10 o'clock that night by the time my brother and sister-in-law were able to pick us up from the hospital. I was beyond ready to get inside, settle the baby, and crash into bed.

But the sweet young teen who was watching the children thought it would be fun for all of them to be awake to greet us! I missed my boys terribly, but I was not ready for, nor wanting, to walk into late-night chaos.

I must be a terrible mother!

Of course, they were so excited to see me and to meet their baby sister, and so for quite some time, what seemed like hours, I sat in a small armchair with a baby in my arms, and each boy squeezed up next to me on either side.

I don't know if I can do this!
I don't know how to do this!
I have to do this!
I will do this!

I was so incredibly bone tired! The next night would be another late one, as my husband arrived by a bus sometime after midnight. It was crazy late. I was still crazy tired and crazy weak, but I was equally crazy relieved that my man was back where he belonged.

To put into perspective what effect the events of the last few weeks had on my health, I needed only to compare my post-pregnancy health this time with the other two. During this pregnancy, I had gained just sixteen pounds. Two weeks after she was born, I had lost those 16 pounds plus another ten. I lost twenty-six pounds in two weeks!

However, I gave no thought to the fact that I had been through a difficult pregnancy, traumatic birth, surgery, and separation from my husband during a very difficult ordeal. I did not even consider that this weight loss was not healthy. Just the opposite, I considered it to be a bright spot in all the darkness I had been through.

It would be about a year before I felt stronger. For years, I had been oblivious to the reality of my physical, mental, and emotional health, and this ordeal did nothing to change that.

My husband would come and go often during the first few months after our daughter's birth. The away six weeks, home two weeks; away three months, home one month; away four months, home three weeks was the unpredictable rotation of his sea duty tours for most of his career.

The coming and going has its own set of difficulties. Just as I was getting a routine that worked well for the kids and me, he would return home, and the order of things would naturally change. During the first week at home, I would adjust to sharing parenting and sharing decisions. The second week had us preparing for the upcoming deployment. This back and forth wreaks havoc on family life.

I found it very difficult to adjust to the mental and emotional roller-coaster ride that was our life. When our daughter was but a couple of months old, our sailor was once again on deployment. I was in the commissary (the military grocery store) with all three of my littles.

The baby was in the front of the cart in an infant carrier. My sweet boys were walking next to and holding onto each side of the cart. They knew that they were to hold on and touch nothing. And that's exactly what they did. A lovely older woman approached me and said something that has stayed with me since.

"You are doing wonderfully," she said softly as she touched my arm lightly.

I was actually taken aback, but I thanked her and felt myself standing a bit taller and feeling more confident and less overwhelmed. It did wonders for my fragile psyche. I determined then and there that I, too, would be that older woman encouraging mothers of young ones.

One positive comment can speak to someone for years to

come! Our words, helpful or hurtful, are so very powerful. I choose to be the example that this dear older woman was to me those 40+ years ago: a voice of encouragement.

Why, though, is it so often easier to be that voice for others than for ourselves?

Chapter 14

BFFs For Life

We moved into naval base housing in October 1978. Most days and many nights were spent with our friends and family. We shared meals, and we shared our lives. Our children were in the same age ranges and played non-stop together. I learned how to cross-stitch from my sister-in-law and upped my sewing game with my best friend. To this day, I still very much enjoy both.

I honestly believe we were living our lives much like the early church in the sense that we were growing together. Not trying to be, just being.

We were so truly blessed by each other. Our husbands did car repairs together. We helped out with each other's kids. On more than one occasion, one of us would go with the other in the middle of the night to the naval hospital because one of our children was suffering terribly from an ear infection.

My sister-in-law and I spent our days together and prepared meals together frequently. Our favorite meal was cold chicken pie. We probably made it once a week, especially in the summer. We haven't had it in years, but it might be making a comeback in our kitchen soon.

I watched their children when my friend was able to fly to Italy for a rendezvous with her sailor, and she did the same for me. We even have old photos of the eight littles (our three, our friend's three, and my sister-in-law's two) lined up in the bathtub. We were family! Other than that of my high school best friend, we shared a bond beyond anything I had ever known. We needed each other, and we were there for each other.

I could not then, nor can I now, imagine how I would have gotten through what we would soon be facing. As I learned earlier, God knows what we need and whom we need!

Chapter 15

We Share Everything

With promotions came pay increases. Sometime after we were unable to pay the $16 to the hospital, a pay raise came to us. That pay increase afforded us the ability to trade the Impala in for a new Datsun 210 station wagon. It was a great little car for our family, and we drove it for several years before having a mechanical problem.

Since the car was past the coverage period and we did not want the expense of having it in a shop, the guys set out to find the problem. Because both families owned a Datsun (I told you we did a lot together), they took the running carburetor apart to compare it to ours, which was not working. It took days to inspect each part and compare it before discovering the issue. It was a speck of lint that was clogging it. I imagine a shop would not have done that and probably would have replaced something that didn't need to be done. Their diligence in this was a testimony to their perseverance and tenacity.

Those same character traits would serve them well in the

United States Navy. To our good fortune, they would rarely be away from home at the same time. Each would stand in for the other when home repairs were needed, and home repairs are always needed when your spouse is gone. It's just the norm.

It was a tremendous blessing to each family. We continued to get together for meals and such, even when one or the other was deployed.

Once in a while, the three of us would go to lunch or dinner. One such time found the three of us seated with my husband between us two ladies. You have to know my friend and understand her naivety to appreciate the many times she will say something, and everyone but her appreciates the humor. I still marvel at our server's ability to remain straight-faced when my friend ordered one dessert and three forks. Again, my husband sitting between the two of us, she blurts out,

"We're best friends. We share everything!"

When my husband returned early from deployment, and I was out of town, he called her to ask to be picked up. Her husband was out to sea at the time. After driving across the flight line (a serious no-no), she walked into his squadron and announced, "I'm here to pick up (my husband's name). His wife is out of town!"

And that is how rumors get started!

These light-hearted moments are a welcome relief from the difficult, often arduous, separations that are a necessary part of military life. We came through one such arduous separation very early in my husband's career.

Chapter 16

Shore Duty/Sea Duty/ Call of Duty

My husband's duty rotation was typically three years of Shore Duty followed by three years of Sea Duty. There are times when Shore Duty will be shortened to fill a necessary certification or make rank, among other reasons.

Most Navy members serve Sea Duty exactly as the name infers, at sea. These sailors are known as "Black Shoes." As the name implies, they wear black shoes. The Naval Air members are known as "Brown Shoes." My husband was a brown shoe. His entire naval career was in helicopter squadrons. Most of his time was spent in squadrons of the largest helicopters in the United States military at that time.

This fact would be the reason his squadron, during a three-year Sea Duty rotation, was called to duty in the fall of 1979. A military member is on duty 24-7, 365 days every year, to serve and defend at a moment's notice for any reason. Whether you are on Sea Duty or Shore Duty, you are always on Call of Duty.

I knew all of this in theory, but we had not been a military family for very long, and I was young and naive about many things.

On the day he called me about leaving the next morning, it honestly had not occurred to me that this would ever happen. After all, he was not a Navy Seal, Army Ranger, or any other kind of Special Forces.

But I was certainly given fair warning with the birth of our daughter that he could and would be expected to answer the call of duty based on his country's needs and his commitment to do so, and my military man would do so without hesitation.

As I said, I was still quite naive. I would not remain so much longer.

Chapter 17

Nobody Consulted Me

lthough it is cliché, it is no less true that we all remember exactly where we were and what we were doing when something shocking in our world happens. It's as if everything comes to a complete halt while we collectively process the event.

This same sensation can take place on an individual level. It did so in my little world on that beautiful, sunny, and crisp fall day in 1979. It was not yet noon, and I had already cleaned the house and packed suitcases for our short getaway. I loved coming home to a clean house.

We were leaving in the morning, and I was so excited to be heading to Philadelphia to celebrate my grandfather's 90th birthday. Many in my family had not yet even met my husband, much less our three littles. I was in great spirits when, as I finished mopping the kitchen floor, the wall phone rang.

"Hello?" I am one of those folks who answer the phone with a question.

"I need you to wash all my clothes. I'm leaving in the morning."

It was his voice, but his words were so matter-of-fact, lacking emotion.

What he was saying made absolutely no sense.

I chuckle.

He doesn't.

"But we're leaving for the party tomorrow!" I replied with my voice full of emotion.

"Not now. My leave's been canceled," oh so very monotone.

"I'm leaving in the morning, and I need you to wash all my clothes," he repeats.

"Where are you going?"

"I don't know."

"When will you be back?"

"I don't know."

Okay, this is just nonsense. What's the punchline?

Of course, I knew there was none. My husband was not a jokester. He would become a gentler and more empathetic husband in the future, but this was his way of processing the news and was all he could offer at the time.

He was doing what was absolutely necessary to comply with his orders by focusing on the facts. I was doing what was necessary to make sense of it all by being in denial.

"I'll be home shortly," he said with a hint of excitement in his voice.

"I'll start the laundry."

And while I am doing so, I will be very confused and very angry and very hurt that you don't seem to even care about how I feel!

I do not remember very much about that night except that very little conversation took place. What would be the point? I had a zillion questions, and he had zero answers. At least none that he could or would share with me.

I will never forget, however, him kneeling beside each of our children's beds, praying and crying as I stood in the bedroom doorways, watching and doing the same.

Little to no sleep was afforded to either of us that night. I would spend the entire night feeling abandoned. He would spend it, for the most part, imagining what this call to serve would involve. At least, that was what I determined because he was not talking about it or much of anything else.

The emotional toll of separation, whether expected or totally unexpected, is experienced differently for the service member and the spouse. I didn't realize all of that at the time.

It was becoming very clear to me that my husband was, first and foremost, dedicated to the service of his country. It was who he was. I would take a back seat from time to time, and so would our children.

The fact that he was leaving on orders from his employer, the United States of America, did not hurt as much as my perception that he did not dread the unknown of what lies ahead nearly as much as I did. I suppose it was some sort of irrational and unfair judgment on my part, but it was how I felt nonetheless.

Chapter 18

The First Two Weeks

Several hours before we were supposed to be on the road as a family, we were a family dropping the daddy off at his squadron. He would fly out to who knows where to do who knows what for who knows how long.

The ride home was tough, to say the least. They sat in the back seat, oblivious, sweet, and happy kiddos just enjoying the early morning outing while their mommy, feeling scared, alone, overwhelmed, sad, and mad, was trying and failing to keep it all together. Tears like rain poured all the way home.

In future deployments, we would learn that a couple of weeks leading up to it are so angst-filled that you find yourself counting down the days of the departure so that you can finally start counting down the days of the return.

I think of this time as the emotional separation before the physical separation. Emotions are raw, and arguments pop up easily and last too long. You are wishing away the little time you have together so that you can begin looking forward to the reunion.

I believe it is a subconscious effort to emotionally separate yourself from your partner in an attempt to make the physical separation less painful. It is a bizarre phenomenon, and it cannot be avoided. Also, it doesn't work.

But there was no lead-up to this deployment. No emotional separation. No arguments.

No conversation at all to speak of. There was no return date. There would be no countdown. There was no time for my psyche to work through the emotions, but I would still have to work through them and many others for an unforeseen length of time.

I did not understand any of this at the time. I was just trying to do what I needed to do to take care of our children and protect them from my fragile emotional state.

I was desperately seeking God!

I had no idea if or when I would hear from my husband. My days were filled with caring for my littles, talking to our friends, and watching television for any clue what was going on and how he might be involved. I was pretty much in a constant state of anxiety. He knew where he was. He knew what he was doing. But I had no idea of either, and I had no idea when I would know.

My days were busy, thankfully, but everything I did was half-hearted and lacking focus. For the sake of the children, I kept emotions pent up during the day. But the tears would flow at night in our cold, lonely bed.

If I could just hear from him, then I would be okay.

My heart raced every time the phone rang.

As often as I had prayed for it, I was caught completely off guard when the only call I cared about finally came to me.

"Hello?" I nonchalantly asked, expecting it to be anyone but him.

Delay and static.

"Hey! Before you say anything, our call is being monitored. I cannot tell you anything, and if you even ask a question, we will be disconnected." He sounded so good!

Delay and static.

"Are you okay?"

Delay and static.

"I'm fine. How are you and the kids?" Delay and static.

"We're good. We miss you so much!"

Delay and static

"Miss you all so much too. Gotta go. I love you."

Call ended!

I love you too.

Still no answers but peace of mind knowing he was okay. Still had no idea where he was. Still had no idea what he was doing or when I'd hear from him again. But he sounded good, and I would hold on to that thought. It was the emotional boost I needed.

It was obvious to me and those in my circle that we need only turn the tv on to the nightly news to know what was going on. He had to be somehow involved in the Iranian Hostage Crisis. But how or why was just the opposite of obvious.

I received notification of a meeting for all squadron spouses where explanations would be given. I walked into the large, crowded room and took a seat toward the back. I may have known a couple of wives well enough to recognize them if I saw them, but I did not see anyone familiar, and I wasn't in the mood to socialize anyway. After several minutes of introductions, we were informed that our husbands were on a ship in the Indian Ocean. Everyone should be hearing from their loved ones via mail soon—end of meeting.

I left without speaking to anyone. I left being privy to something that no one else seemed to be aware of. I might not have known where my husband was, but I certainly knew where he was not. Some of the squadron might have been on a ship in the Indian Ocean, but he most certainly was not on a ship anywhere.

He would not have been able to call me from a ship.

Chapter 19

Fish Out of Water

When two more weeks passed with no further word from my husband, the emotional boost from the strange phone call was waning. I decided to make the trip back home for Thanksgiving as planned. It would be good to be with family and for the kids to be with all their cousins.

As tempting as it was to stay around in case he called, I decided to get away for a while. I would get a chance to talk to his brother, who had recently gotten out of the Navy. He had actually been in the same squadron as my husband, so he should have some good insight.

There was no such thing as a small gathering in my husband's family. His parents, his eleven siblings, spouses of those married, and the oh-so-many children made Thanksgiving 1979 the normal gathering, with one exception. The third oldest was not there, and none of us knew where he was.

As good as it was to be with everyone and pick my brother-in-law's brain, the distraction was not enough to keep my mind off my missing man.

Where was he?

What was he doing?

Was he safe?

And when, oh when, would I see him again?

Everyone was chatting, laughing, joking around as if all was well in the world.

Do you not realize that our country is involved in a crisis?

Do you not even care that your son, brother, or uncle is missing from this gathering?

Have you even noticed?

Of course, they cared, but I was feeling isolated. No one there could possibly empathize with me to the degree that would bring me any comfort.

It was both understandable and unfair to expect them to do so.

It would not take long for me to feel the overwhelming desire, even need, to get back where I belonged. I needed to get back to where my military family surrounded me—to the place where everyday news was military news.

I would never feel that way again about going back to our hometown. In fact, my heart is still there forty-six years after moving away. But that day, I was a fish out of water, and I only wanted to get back to my fishbowl.

Chapter 20

Thanks, Uncle Sam

T he best Christmas gift I ever received was from Uncle Sam that December. My husband would be coming home for Christmas. He didn't know how long he would be home, but our little family would be together for the first time since early November.

There isn't much that can pull on your heartstrings more than a military homecoming, whether it is celebrating the reunion of 6000 sailors with their families all lined up on the dock and running to each other all at once or a simple, joyful occasion of one family reunited after an unexpected separation.

Our time together was precious and absolutely not taken for granted for one minute. I was pretty much stuck like glue to my fella once the kids were in bed. Until then, he was all theirs.

It turned out that he would be home for two weeks before the call came that he was to return. During those two weeks, not one word was spoken about where he'd been or what he'd been doing. If I thought he would tell me, I would have pulled out my list of never-ending questions, but I knew better than that. Truthfully, his devotion to our country and his excellent character were two of the traits that I so loved about him.

As it turned out, by the time he retired from the Navy, he would have always been home for Christmas, which is extremely unusual for the military in general and all but unheard of for the Navy.

Once our Christmas celebration was over, the reality of the unknown was once again at the forefront of my mind. The emotional toll would find me dealing with 'demons' that had been with me for many years. Some had such a strong hold on me that it would be many years before I understood the correlation between my emotional and physical states.

I began controlling the only thing I believed I could. My food intake or lack thereof. Of course, this was not a conscious decision on my part. It was not the first time, nor would it be the last.

Chapter 21

The Weight of It All

I began having migraines and digestive issues as early as grade school. It was not an everyday occurrence, but it was often. Migraines (simply called headaches at the time) were quite common for me. Foods, emotions, scents, stress, and even weather patterns were among the triggers. I know that now. But no one paid attention to any of those things at that time. I was given aspirin and put to bed with a warm washcloth on my forehead. That was all that was known for treating "headaches" then. They can also be hereditary. My dad had terrible ones too. Some of my siblings and some of my grandchildren do too.

I can remember every migraine I have had. They are memorable events. I think I took aspirin every day, or most days, my entire teenage years. I either had a headache or what I call the "threat of a headache" almost every single day.

They subsided somewhat during my twenties and thirties but returned with a vengeance in my forties. The two worst ones were actually caused by medication. I was following the medication instructions that read to take two, and if the headache is still present in three hours, take two more. If still present in three more hours, take two more. The pain continued to worsen with each dose until I was pacing our living room while the top of my head felt like it was going to explode. I knew I just had to wait it out, so for hours, I paced.

The second one started as what is called a rebound migraine. Sometimes, when you have many headaches in a short period of time, each headache brings on another headache. The same thing can happen when medication is taken too often, except much more painful and long-lasting. Some can last for days. One particular migraine event that I dealt with was felt in my eye. Again, I knew I had to wait it out without pain meds, so I laid in bed for two days with what felt like dozens of needles drilling into my eye.

These always brought me to God. Pain has a way of doing that. God used migraines to remind me of His presence. He does not always remove our pain in the timely manner that we seek, but He is with us during it. He faithfully uses it all to draw us to Himself. His Word is true.

"It was good for me to be afflicted so that I might learn your decrees." (*Psalms 119:71*)

I am incredibly thankful that, after years of dealing with them, I no longer experience migraines. As all migraine sufferers know, each episode leaves you completely exhausted. So, even a migraine that lasts a few hours can affect you for several days.

Thankfully, I have not experienced a single migraine for several years by taking a natural supplement every night at bedtime. I do not sell these supplements!

I have also dealt with intestinal issues my whole life. I have read that stress can trigger stomach pain in some folks and headaches in others. Well, for me, it was both!

The intestinal issues were also triggered by years of poor eating habits and stress. I began a quest for something that was not what I needed nor what was best for me.

My quest was rooted deeply in poor self-esteem and embracing the emphasis on outward appearance that was prevalent in my young adult years. Instead of seeking wise counsel (I have no recollection of emotional and mental health issues being addressed), my focus turned to fixing something that was not broken. I was, ironically, breaking it in the process!

I was a physically active child of an ideal healthy weight. I was also extremely shy, self-conscious, and emotional. While I was healthy, I did deal with bouts of constipation. I do not remember talking about it or ever being treated for it.

In my teens, I was athletic and maintained an ideal weight. As most teenagers in the 1960's (think of Twiggy), I was very much aware of body comparisons. I was a bit prideful that I had a good figure and could eat whatever I wanted. What I wanted was junk, mostly.

Fast-food restaurants were few and far between at that time. While I certainly enjoyed healthy meals prepared by my mother, it was not at all uncommon for me to skip lunch at school and then gorge on the chips, candy, and sodas available at our after-school concession.

As soon as I graduated from high school, I began working at a bank processing center from 7:00 p.m. to 3:00 a.m. My social life went from get-togethers and parties with my friends to late-night meals with ladies twice my age. I was miserable, and I was not eating well at all.

I was losing weight. When I woke up with pain in my upper abdomen that felt like someone had punched me, I could not even stand up straight. I was diagnosed with a spastic colon. The pain subsided with medication, and soon afterward, I was fortunate to be hired at a day job. My stomach issue was all but forgotten.

The day I got married, I stood 5 feet 3 inches and weighed 108 pounds. I had yet to give any thought to food intake or calories.

Our first child was born on Labor Day, 1974. I love the irony of that. I never experienced any labor. My water broke around midnight, and upon reaching the maternity ward of the hospital, I was asked how far apart my pains were. I told the nurse that I didn't think I'd had any yet. Much to my surprise and utter delight, I was hooked up to a powerful pain blocker.

It was so strong that even 12 hours after he was born, I still had no feeling from my waist down. Just enough sensation had returned for me to be aware of a strange aching deep inside. I believe it was God who prompted me to mention this to the nurse because, obviously I had no idea what I was supposed to be feeling.

She checked my stomach and, in a panic, let out, "Oh my God, they never put a catheter in. Your bladder is about to burst!"

At that moment, I knew I would never be so completely dependent on others if I could possibly avoid it. It frightened me enough to decide and stick to my decision that I would give birth naturally from then on.

I must have thought on a subconscious level that I would have the baby, and my weight and body shape would magically return to that of pre-pregnancy. When that did not happen, I was thrown into a downward spiral of self-consciousness about my weight for the first time in my life.

I was constantly comparing myself to other women. I was depressed that my pre-pregnancy clothes no longer fit. I am not talking about a huge weight difference. But I was, for the first time in my life, coming to terms with a body that I did not like.

I did lose most of the baby weight, but not as quickly as I expected, and not all of it. After all, I was certain that I would be back to that magical 108 pounds immediately. I lost touch with reality. At the same time, having become a Christian, my whole life was changing at an accelerated rate, and walking in faith is a life-long process. I was slow to recognize the sin of living a self-absorbed life, and I was far from the maturity level needed to see the truth about body image, food choices, and womanhood.

I was also surrounded by women who were all obsessed with weight and body image. I didn't so much fall into the trap as

I jumped into it. I had gained 40 pounds during pregnancy, and my baby was nearing a year old. I had lost down to 120. Weighing this much was uncharted territory, and I just could not accept this strange new me. For the first time in my life, I dieted.

And by diet, I mean that I consumed about 1,000 calories a day. After all but starving myself for a couple of weeks, my weight went down to 113 pounds. Instead of understanding that losing seven pounds in a couple of weeks was far from a healthy weight loss, I was foolishly and immaturely feeling defeated and discouraged that it was not more.

What would I have to do to get back to 108 pounds?

I did not get a chance to find out. I was pregnant with our second when our first was thirteen months old. I was actually relieved that my dieting days were behind me. And I was really hungry! In my mind, pregnancy meant acceptable weight gain. In a bit of a Scarlet O'Hara moment from *Gone With the Wind*, I would worry about that later.

I gained 30 pounds with the second pregnancy. I was aware of my weight, but I was not dieting or obsessing about it. After he was born, I was very unhappy with my weight, but I was not dieting. I would come to realize that my appetite waxed and waned based on my stress levels. My overall health was greatly affected by this, but I did not make the connection then.

When the boys were 2 years old and six months old, and we had become a military family; I decided to join the gym on base and refocus on my weight. I weighed 125 pounds, much more than I had ever weighed, and I was depressed about it.

Just one month after joining the gym, I became pregnant with number three.

Caring for two toddlers while carrying my third baby in as many years left me no time or desire to think about weight. When I was but a few months pregnant, we decided to help out a family member and took into our home her seven- and three-year-old children. It took its toll on me physically and mentally, and I was becoming quite worn down.

I also foolishly decided that since my oldest was two, I must potty train him. This is what all of the parenting magazines told us, and I based most decisions on what others expected, without question. The amount of stress that I put on myself was incredible, but I did not realize it then. Neither he nor I were ready, but that did not stop me. I was driven by doing it, just as the books said. I sure could have used some wise words from older women, but there was none forthcoming at that time. Our precious niece and nephew would be with us for three months.

I was 25 years old and six months pregnant when I flew with the seven-year-old, the three-year-old, my two-year-old, and my 13-month-old by myself. I was fearful of flying and overwhelmed.

At the time, my husband was allowed to board the plane with me and help get the children settled in. I held my baby in my lap for the whole flight. All of the children were angels.

Never once did it occur to me that I was under such stress that I was physically affected by it. I just kept doing all the things required of me and many that were not. It was during this time that a pattern developed that would play out again and again for many years.

When I was upset, mad, hurt, or stressed, my appetite would all but disappear. It would remain suppressed for the duration of the event that triggered it. All too often, this meant weeks at a time.

Once I began eating normally again, I would eat as if I had been starved, which I was to a degree. I was doing it to myself with no thought to the damage it caused. The next big trigger event did not last weeks. It lasted months.

Chapter 22

Groundhog Day -
The Not Funny Version

Remember the 1993 movie *Groundhog Day* with Bill Murray and Andi MacDowell? It was so funny and entertaining that folks still watch it over and over. Ah, the irony! Watching a movie over and over again that is about a day that repeats itself over and over again.

Long before that movie came out, we lived our own, albeit not funny, Groundhog Day experience between November 1979 and April 1980. The scenario became more and more maddening each time it played out.

I know now, we all know now, that the Iranian Hostage Crisis would be dealt a devastating blow by the ill-fated USA hostage rescue mission. For some of us, those long months leading up to it were some of the most difficult months of our lives.

I fed my children well but did not do so for myself. I was again appetite-suppressed. My man would come home from time to time. We never knew when that would be or how long he would be home. At some point, he would receive a call to leave the next day again. So, while he was home, we were on edge, awaiting the inevitable call.

I would go from single parenting to sharing the parenting role, which was not always easy. His heart was with us, but his head was not always. There was, of course, always the elephant in the room, and oh, how I hated that elephant!

Each time he came home, it was for an undisclosed period of time, only to return to the mission for an undisclosed period of time. Of course, I had no idea where he was going or when he would be back. I was back to single parenting.

How did I do this before?

There were phone calls and only occasional letters filled with nothing but nothing. Upon receipt of one such letter, I was so angry and frustrated and tired of it all that I tore up the letter, stomped into the garage, slammed the door shut, picked up a bucket, and threw it as hard as I could into the door. It didn't help! Well, it helped a little!

Voila! He would return home again for another visit. That's all it was by this point. How nice that he came home for a short visit. Sarcasm intended. We never left the house together because someone must be there to answer the phone summoning his return.

Cell phones had not even been thought of. It was like being imprisoned in your own home. That may sound a bit overly dramatic, but after several months of this back-and-forth, seemingly never-ending saga, it felt very much that way.

One particularly disturbing event that took place while he was away was a phone call that went something like this . . .

"Hello?" I asked.

"What size bra do you wear?" the eerie voice asked.

I was shocked and could not speak.

"I'm guessing it's . . . " he continued with the correct answer!

I slammed the phone down as hard as I could and sat there imagining some strange man in my bedroom, rifling through my undergarment drawer.

Oh my! What if he even took something with him?

What if he comes back while the kids and I are here?

What if he is a serial rapist or something?

I certainly did not sleep well that night.

I would hear from him again.

I was hesitant to answer any call after that. Like cell phones, caller ID was a thing of the future. I had determined that if I did hear back from him, I knew exactly what I would say, and I prayed that my words would be backed by the power of the Holy Spirit.

When he did indeed call back, I did not understand what he was saying, but I firmly interrupted him, saying,

"I rebuke you in the name of Jesus Christ, and I command you to never call here again!"

I slammed the phone down, sat on the edge of the bed, shaking and crying and asking God to scare the mess out of him.

He must have because I never heard from him again.

My husband would later learn that one of the young men

in the squadron was making these phone calls to some of the spouses of the deployed service members. Thank God, at least he wasn't a serial rapist—that we knew of.

Each time my husband left, I would sink deeper into my pit of despair. I have asked my kids, and they have assured me they had absolutely no idea I was struggling. They were so young that, thankfully, they have no memory of it whatsoever.

My oldest doesn't even remember sitting next to me on our couch during a break-down that I was unsuccessful in hiding from him. He reached out, patting my hand and telling me that he would take care of me. My eyes are tear-filled remembering this.

The truth is that my children were what kept me going. I would not, could not, lose control. They deserved the full attention, love, nurturing, and parenting of the only one they had with them.

Ah, but at night, the tears would flow, and the prayers would go forth. I fell asleep with the doubts, the fears, the loneliness, and all of the unknowns as my nightly companions.

I still have dreams to this day that my husband is gone with the military, and he cannot call me. The dreams play out differently, but the theme is the same. He is gone, we cannot talk, and I do not know when he will be home. I am always relieved to wake up and look over and touch him.

Each time he left, I became more anxious about what exactly he was doing. I knew it was dangerous, and that was all I needed to know to keep my imagination fueled. I remember quite clearly, not too long after my temper tantrum in the garage; I was in our bedroom listening to the most recent list of catastrophic events that my imagination had conjured up.

My prayers must be falling on deaf ears.

I had been asking, pleading with God to bring this to an end. I was certain that I would be a widow at the age of 27 with three little ones.

"Do You even care about that?" I implored Him.

"Do You even care about my kids and me?" I questioned.

My rant toward God continued for quite some time until I fell to my knees, collapsed, and whispered, "God, I give it all to you. I am so very weary of all the wrestling. I give my husband to you. Have your will, Father, even if that means that he will die. I trust You and give my whole situation over to You for Your purpose."

After praying these words, I would enter into a place of peace, free of fear for the first time in such a very long time. It was not the first nor would it be the last time that God would lead me to His Word once I was truly listening.

> "Do not be anxious about anything, but in every situation, by prayer and petition, with thanksgiving, present your requests to God. And the peace of God, which transcends all understanding, will guard your hearts and your minds in Christ Jesus." *(Phil. 4:6-7)*

There would be many challenges in the future where I would again be reminded of this truth. Still, He graciously granted it to me for the duration of this particular personal crisis during this particular national crisis.

With peace in my mind and spirit, my appetite once again picked up. I was completely oblivious to the connection and would remain that way while more and more damage was being done to my physical health. Depriving myself of the necessary nourishment for extended periods of time, followed by eating that was fueled by feelings of well-being, left my body constantly adjusting and re-adjusting.

Chapter 23

Diet, Discipline, and Discipleship

Over the years, I bounced back and forth between my own dieting plans and structured ones. I joined one such structured diet, *Diet, Discipline and Discipleship* in the 1980's when we spent several months back in our hometown. It was a wonderful program with common sense food plans and weekly scripture memorization, as well as weekly meetings.

I came to learn much later in life that pretty much any diet will work for the purpose of losing weight. If you do not continue with it for the rest of your life, which is all but impossible, you will be right back where you started. Or in my case and so many others' I'm sure, you will be much worse off than before you started.

I weighed 120 pounds when I started the program. I had been maintaining this healthy weight for several years. Because one of the weekly requirements of the program was a weigh in, I was mentally and emotionally thrown back into focusing on myself and my body image. The required weigh-in was witnessed by two of the ladies leading the group.

Again, since losing weight was an important element, I believed I must do so. It was expected. I convinced myself that these ladies must see that I could lose weight and thus be successful in the program. Ego and pride were once again in the forefront, the exact opposite purpose of the study!

I can't remember how long the study lasted, but my weight did go down to 113 pounds, and I was quite proud of that. I'm sure I ate a much more restricted diet than planned.

Scenarios such as this played out again and again. Each time I would follow a restrictive food regimen, full-on eating whatever I wanted. Even when I did use some discipline and implemented much of what I had learned along the way, I would gain weight more readily with each passing diet plan. I had been in and out of this weight loss and weight gain cycle for years.

At this point, it had been about five years since the Iranian Hostage ordeal. I had welcomed its abrupt ending for my own selfish reasons, but for my husband, this was far from the case.

Chapter 24

The Devastating News

In mid-April, shortly after heading back to wherever he would go, my husband was returned home to have his ankle checked out. He was having some issues from the softball injury a few years earlier, and they wanted him to have it looked at.

The day before he was to return to the training, the ill-fated Iranian Hostage Crisis attempted rescue took place. It was devastating news for our entire country but so much more for the families of the eight brave servicemen who gave their lives.

While details of the failed mission were years from being disclosed, I now knew what I had suspected was true. My husband had been training for these months for the exact mission. The mission that, as God would have it, took place while he was home. It is all a bit too much to comprehend on a personal level, even these many years later.

Relief and thankfulness consumed me.

Loss and emptiness consumed him.

He drifted into survivor's guilt. He had lost friends in Viet Nam ten years earlier, and now the loss of these men, his friends and fellow servicemen, that he came to know well, shared meals with, and spent days and nights training with were gone.

He was supposed to be with them on the mission. He was ready to put into action all that he had trained for these past many months. Would he have lost his life if he'd gone? It was a question that could not be answered. It would take him a while to come out of the depression.

It was one of only two times in our marriage that I would be by his side as he battled anxiety and depression, but this would be the only time in his Naval career that he would do so.

He was 30 years old but had lived a lifetime's worth of mental and physical stress. I would be with him, caring for him, and giving him the time he needed to move forward. Healing is a process that looks different to each of us. We do heal over time, but we are left with parts and pieces of the aftermath that become a part of who we are.

We would both battle major anxiety again, but that battle would come many years later.

One year after the tragic, failed mission, we attended a memorial in Washington, DC. It was therapeutic for him to be with many of the men he had recently shared half a year with. Meeting some of the relatives of the fallen was an honor. There have been many theories shared about what went wrong in the desert that night, and much can and should be gained from hindsight.

Books have been written and movies made, but theories and books and movies cannot depict the turmoil that each military member and each family member experiences when their daily lives are affected by circumstances that are completely out of their control.

This is true for civilians, first responders, and the military alike. But I believe that the percentage of such is certainly much higher for the military. Sadly, the military boasts more divorces than any other occupation. As a believer, I know that God Himself ministered to our family throughout our twenty-four-year military commitment.

Many years after the Iranian Hostage Rescue Mission, my friend started a military support group in our church. It was a wonderful ministry that I believe would greatly benefit military communities around the world. If I had been part of such a group during our ordeal, I imagine that my kids and I most certainly would have benefitted.

I am so very grateful that we did have that support in our own small circle of friends, but ours may have been the exception. My hope is that it is the rule in most military communities now. No one quite understands the military family life like those living it.

There would be many more separations and angst-filled days leading up to those separations. There would be many more countdowns to homecomings. Our children would sacrifice time with their dad again and again.

Because God is faithful, all our children have grown into responsible, caring, loving, faithful spouses and parents.

. . . For I know the plans I have for you," declares the LORD, "plans to prosper you and not to harm you, plans to give you hope and a future." (*Jer. 29:11*)

Chapter 25

Anxiety to the Max

In the summer of 2004, my husband had retired from the United States Navy and was working full-time with a military contracting company. I was in Canada, helping our daughter, who was pregnant, with her first child. She was on bed rest.

I use the word "helping" loosely. Although I would beat myself up for lying in bed with her way more than helping with anything, I now understand why. I was simply exhausted.

I had yet to heal from the toll that stress had been taking on me for many years. I was going back and forth between working full-time and part-time. My heart was in my home with my children, three grands (and the one on the way). I longed to be free to spend as much time with all of them as possible.

I resented that a job was robbing me of that. My physical and mental health were still suffering, yet I had no clue. Once during this time, when we drove to Canada, I slept the entire twelve hours. I would wake up and go right back to sleep. I could not stay awake and could not understand why I was so tired. Obviously, whenever I could stop, relax, and rest, my body and mind would shut down.

While there during her pregnancy, I developed bronchitis which became pneumonia. These illnesses, too, were my frequent unwanted visitors brought on by all the same triggers affecting my headaches and gut issues. Still, I never put any of this together. It never occurred to me that bronchitis and pneumonia began to plague me after several years of stressful events. I was sick several times a year with one or both. This was so frequent that, at one point, I wondered if it was actually more psychological than physical because my husband always took such wonderful care of me. I wondered if I was bringing it on myself just to be pampered. I remembered that Jim Henson of Muppets fame had passed away from pneumonia several years earlier. When I found myself battling it again for the fourth time in a year, I decided to dig deeper into the causes.

I was tested for allergies and found to be highly allergic to mold. I began allergy shots, and in time, both chronic illnesses ceased to attack my lungs. I do have mild asthma that has been well-managed for many years now.

Before that time came, though, I found myself once again sick in bed at my pregnant daughter and son-in-law's home. Their family doctor had prescribed a powerful antibiotic, and I was resting when I overheard my daughter on the phone. Her voice was shaking, and she was crying! As I was slowly getting up to check on her, she brought me the phone.

It was our oldest son. My husband was in the hospital for a heart problem. He didn't have any details. We were immediately on the phone booking my flight home. Sick or not, I had to get home as soon as possible. First thing the next morning, I was on my way. As soon as I got to the hospital room, I climbed into the bed and curled up next to my husband. The details of why he was there came to light.

He had been in the backyard mowing when he felt that he was going to pass out. As soon as he pushed the mower away, he went down. He had no idea how long he laid there before coming to, making his way into the house, and lying on the floor under the ceiling fan. In time, he made his way upstairs, showered, and went to bed with intention of going to church in the morning.

When he still did not feel well the next morning, he called our son and told him the same and that he would not be at church. After church, our son's family dropped by to check on him. He assured them he was feeling a bit better but mentioned nothing about the previous day's incident.

He went to work that Monday and felt fine. On Tuesday morning, he stopped to put some things in the mail on his way to work. He felt his heart begin to race. He knew not to go back home because there was no one there, but instead of calling for an ambulance or heading to the hospital, he went to work.

His heart continued to race for a couple of hours, and his co-workers became concerned by his skin color and his inability to speak without gasping. For reasons that even he did not understand, he did not want them to call 911. He asked a good friend to take him to the hospital. His friend would tell us later that he thought my husband was going to die before they got there.

He made his way to the check-in, where he saw only one person. As soon as he mentioned that he might be having a heart attack, he was surrounded by people who appeared out of nowhere and had him lying flat on a hospital gurney. He was rushed into the cardiac emergency room, where the paddles were applied to his chest to bring the heart's rhythm down to normal. His heart had been beating at 250 beats per minute for about three hours. A normal resting heart rate is between 60-100 beats per minute. He was admitted to the hospital for tests. After a day, he was moved by ambulance to the heart hospital for care. He was diagnosed with ventricular tachycardia.

They determined that a procedure called an ablation would be done to cause some scarring on the inside of the heart to help break up the electrical signals that cause irregular heartbeats. The procedure was attempted but was not successful. In fact, it was not even completed. His heart stopped twice during the procedure; thus, the decision to discontinue was made.

What happened next is something he prefers to forget. During the procedure, six catheters were placed through his groin up to his heart. Typically, these are removed while the patient is still under anesthesia. But in his case, there was no time to remove them. They were removed one at a time with nothing to block the pain. He shook uncontrollably through the forty-five-minute ordeal.

Shortly thereafter, a defibrillator/pacemaker was inserted in his chest near his heart, and he started two oral medications. This device serves as an internal heart pacer. It also delivers a shock to the heart if the heart rate rises above a programmed number.

Not long after it was in place, he received a shock from the device. Over the next several months, he continued to be shocked by the device several times. The oral medications were changed. Still more shocks. It is said that each shock feels like being kicked by a donkey in the chest. Another ablation was attempted, and although his heart did not stop during the procedure, the procedure nonetheless was unsuccessful. One night shortly after that, he was not feeling well and was sure it was his heart, so our oldest drove us to the naval hospital.

As soon as we made the turn onto the base toward the emergency room, his defibrillator began shocking him. It shocked him twenty or more times in the two minutes that it took to drive up to the front of the ER. He was screaming in pain. Our son jumped out and ran inside to get help. I was in the backseat in an absolute panic. There was a child lock in place, and I was reaching across the front seat to try to unlock it. About the time I got it opened, our son was coming back.

The emergency room was being reconfigured, and nothing was as we expected. In what seemed like hours (of course, it was a matter of minutes), doctors and nurses were at the car and getting my husband onto the gurney; all the while, the defibrillator kept firing.

By this time, I was in meltdown mode. I could not believe my ears when the nurse was clutching my shoulders, telling me to calm down and sternly informing me that I needed to move our vehicle! I looked straight at her, shaking, and just as sternly replied, "I can't calm down, and I don't care what happens to the car!" I may have used an unkind word or two.

I was escorted to a sitting area in the hallway and was joined within minutes by our son, who had just parked the car. I was rocking back and forth and crying. As they wheeled my husband into a room within view, our eyes locked for just a few seconds. We both processed, at the exact same time, the thought that we may never see each other again.

He had been in the room quite some time when the hospital chaplain approached my son and me and kneeled beside me. Before I was able to lose what bit of self-control I held onto, he kindly and softly assured me that my husband was okay, that they were still trying to stabilize him, and that the staff thought I might benefit from a visit with the chaplain.

I was an emotional mess. We were able to go in eventually. There was blood all over the floor where the IV repeatedly came out due to the defibrillator shocks each time they tried to put it in. He was very pale, totally exhausted, and traumatized. But he was alive! He was hospitalized while his cardiac surgeon considered where to go from there. He had an out-of-town surgeon assist him in yet another attempted ablation. It failed. They determined that the type of tachycardia my husband was dealing with was unlike others that follow a circular path around the heart. His was completely erratic and unpredictable.

Therefore, it was impossible to correct. We were sent to Johns Hopkins Heart Hospital. His doctor explained that it was not that doctors there knew something they did not or that they had more technology at their disposal but simply because it was another set of eyes.

My husband, our son, and I spent an hour or more with the head of the Johns Hopkins Heart Hospital, only to be told that he knew of nothing that would help. Everything that could be done had been done, and he was probably looking at having a heart transplant.

The three of us, trying to process this outcome, turned to leave when the doctor asked us to wait. He asked his assistant to show him the EKG once again. He sat silently for five minutes or more, staring at the paper.

He looked back at us and said, "I think I see what is going on here. Your heart also has an extra beat pattern. I think it's very possible that the device is reading the extra beat as tachycardia and administering the shock each time."

His words, "We need to replace your device with one that has two wires," were music to our ears.

We did not have to understand what that meant to be incredibly thankful. We told him over and over again just how thankful we were and left with a huge weight lifted from us. My husband did receive the new device, and we are so happy that this one has not shocked him once in the seven years since it was implanted. Another set of eyes is exactly what made the difference!

However, shortly after the night of the seemingly never-ending defibrillator shocks, we both attended a group for PTSD for several weeks. This ordeal brought on a level of anxiety he had never known. Not from wars, not from failed missions, not from anything life had thrown at him, and I was right there with him. Because just as the military member and the military spouse experience the same event differently, it is also true for the patient and the loved ones.

While we have come far emotionally and he physically, my husband still takes antianxiety meds due to those years of fear and uncertainty. We do know that God has always been and always will be with us, no matter what lies ahead.

". . . for the Lord your God goes with you; he will never leave you nor forsake you." (*Deut. 31:6*)

Chapter 26

No Separations
By Choice

Throughout my husband's career, we dealt with more separations than I can count. I don't know that it was a conscious decision on my part, but going on girl trips or visiting family and friends out of town without him was something I never had the desire to do when my husband was home.

I knew a lot of women who did, and that's okay. But for me, since we dealt with so many separations—not of our choosing—the last thing we wanted was to be apart by choice.

One morning, just after the end of a separation, we were having breakfast together at a local restaurant. After we had been there for quite a while, a man whom we knew from church approached us. Unnoticed by us, he had been sitting a few tables away. He wanted to tell us how he was touched by the way we were completely focused on each other. He said it was as if no one else was even in the restaurant. He was really moved by our obvious love for one another.

Of course, we were unaware that we were being watched and unaware that our affection for each other was obvious to others. I will say that one very bright spot in all the unwanted separations is the many second honeymoon experiences. Just as the original honeymoon ended and real life began, so would our many second honeymoons. But to be blessed with so many special moments is much needed and much appreciated, a bit like making a little lemonade out of those many lemons.

Chapter 27

Life is Full of Adventures

While this memoir focuses on our military challenges, frightening health scares, and my own personal challenges, we did enjoy much more fun times, laughs, fellowship, and bonding than difficulties. Life is full of adventures if we allow ourselves to live some of it off-the-cuff.

One such off-the-cuff adventure occurred in the summer of 1983. Our friends bought an old van to customize for our two-family vacation. For weeks, the guys worked every night and on weekends getting ready for our trip to Canada. None of us had ever been to Canada. We had read that the provincial parks were incredible, and we were going to find the perfect one! So, with the van ready to go, the four of us and the six kids, ages 3 to 9, piled in and hit the road.

The camper was set up with game tables and drink holders, so we were traveling in style. Seat belts were not required then, and the kids played, rolled around, and sat on the comfy, carpeted floor. We did absolutely no planning. We were on an adventure, and part of the thrill was figuring everything out as we went. At least, that's what we tell ourselves now.

In reality, we just weren't very smart. After a fun stop at Niagara Falls, we headed to the provincial park that we had imaged as a sort of Canadian Shangri-La. Had we done even a little planning, we would have learned that July 1 is a Canadian holiday and provincial parks are impossible to enter.

We found this out when we rolled up to one late at night. The park ranger explained this to us and was sorry to inform us that there was no room in the camp. The best he could offer was directions to a private camping ground quite a distance from there that might have space for us.

It was past midnight when we drove down the long dirt road in pitch black until we came to what appeared to be the check-in cabin. It was brightly lit, and there was quite a party going on inside. Although they did not technically have any spots available, they could show us the way to an area we could set up. Canadians really are like that. Welcoming and accommodating.

We never could have imagined on that first visit in 1983 that many of the folks nearest and dearest to our hearts are Canadians. We have visited often since that late July 1 night.

It was actually July 2 by the time we rolled in, and our escort greeted us. With no warning, the side door flew open, a young man jumped in, and while hanging onto the door jamb, he began shouting directions through the dark forest.

It seemed like a never-ending ride to the end of civilization in the dark. Once we reached our destination (we knew this only because he said so), he had our friend turn off the lights. You could not see your hand in front of your face. He had him run the van back and forth repeatedly to flatten the 4-foot-high weeds.

Once we got out, we could see a small campfire across the way, surrounded by several folks whose faces we could not make out. They kindly yelled an invitation to join them for some weed and alcoholic beverages, and we politely declined the invite, explaining that we had to set up camp and get our children settled.

As I said, very little planning went into this, including the fact that we had not even put the lantern together. We had no idea how to set up the pop-up tent that the adults would be sleeping in. But all the children were settled in the van safe and sound.

We did only what we absolutely had to do with the flame of a cigarette lighter and then crashed onto our bedding, but very little sleep would come for the adults. Soon, we heard someone running toward us. He was screaming, "Come to Site #_. So-and-so is beating up his old lady."

Oh, my goodness!

What have we gotten ourselves and our children into?

All night long, we heard whooping and hollering at a distance from one side of the campsite and whooping and hollering back from the other side. All night long!

At the first sign of sunlight, we stepped out of our tent to see where we had been escorted the night before. A woman, wearing a halter top and cutoff jeans, stepped out, surrounded by motorcycles, lifted a jug over her shoulder, and took a big swig.

We threw everything back into the van and followed the previous night's tire tracks out of there much faster than we had entered. Our friend was tempted to sit on the horn the whole way out, but that would have been a bad idea for many reasons, but none more so than the fact that we were the ones being welcomed into their world, albeit a very nerve-wracking one for us.

With our one and only private campground stay behind us, we began our search for the perfect campsite at the perfect provincial park. Why we did this, I do not know because we had no idea what that would even look like. My friend's main concern was finding somewhere to plug in her curling iron. We stopped at several gas stations on our quest, and oddly, every single one was flooded. That was truly bizarre.

Even more bizarre, each and every provincial park ladies' restroom came with men. The first one was a young man taking photos of his girlfriend while we were showering. But that was not nearly as disturbing to us as the number of times we encountered male park employees cleaning the ladies' restrooms. We immediately and indignantly reported this to the ranger at the gate, only to be told that it was perfectly acceptable. Well, that was certainly unexpected. It may have been acceptable, but we never accepted it.

Actually, we did. We just tried to plan our visits when the

cleaning had already been done. I laugh now at how we had a sneak peek into the protocols to come.

Our quest for the perfect campsite took us from one park to another. We arrived, set up camp, ate, and slept for one night each time. Then we packed back up after breakfast to make our way to the next one. The kids didn't seem to care one bit.

They loved running around and playing at each and every park. My friend and I spent our time cooking, cleaning, and going to laundromats. Our husbands were incredibly longsuffering through it all. I must add, though, that neither they nor we have ever been camping again! But we do get great laughs still today.

Of the many photos taken, one is of our four-year-old daughter running. The photo captures her in perfect stride. I remember thinking that she had great form and looked like she was going to be athletic. She did end up playing field hockey through highschool, earning a partial sports scholarship to college.

She met a young man who was at the same school on a soccer scholarship. It turns out, he is from Canada, just a few miles from where that picture of our 4-year-old girl was taken. She married him in 2002, and they reside with their son and daughter in Canada today.

His family and friends are the Canadian folks that we so love and consider to be our family and friends as well.

.

Chapter 28

Major (or should I say Captain) Faux Pas

S hortly after the Iranian Hostage Crisis ended, my husband was granted a meritorious promotion. Typically, in the Navy, promotion is earned by a passing test grade on the exam that is based on your rate and time in the previous rank. The meritorious promotion, awarded after his service during the Iranian Hostage Mission, meant that he would not have to take the exam nor complete the time in his current rank.

That same year he was named Sailor of the Year by his command. It is a great honor that includes your name being added to the others for the selection of Sailor of the Year for the entire base.

All candidates and spouses are invited to a dinner honoring them and announcing the overall winner. His honor also came with a designated parking space in front of the squadron offices.

On the day of the dinner, he was at work as usual. My

friend was headed to a pottery factory on the other side of the bridge tunnel with a couple of ladies from her church. She had car problems along the way, and since she was very close to the base, she called my husband and asked if she could borrow his truck and bring it back by the time he was ready to leave work.

She called me later that day to ask if I wanted to go with her to return his truck, but I was actually getting ready for the dinner that night and was not able to go along. She returned his truck to his designated spot and moved to the passenger side. Several folks came out, looked over at her, and nodded.

When we got to the dinner, we sat at the reserved table for my husband and his command leaders and spouses. We sat down, greeted the folks around the table, and began the usual chit-chat. Little time had passed when his commanding officer, a captain in the Navy looked at me and declared, "You're not the woman I saw in your husband's truck earlier."

All chatter around the table stopped.

Wow! That was very unprofessional!

I immediately chuckled and explained the whole story behind the blond sitting in my husband's truck. But I was shocked at just how uncouth he was. My husband told me later that the captain never really liked him, but I can't help but think how terribly out of line he was to confront me with everyone at the table privy to it.

While I did handle it with poise, I have often wondered what he would have done if I acted shocked and angry or had made a scene, disrupting the dinner - but because I have absolutely no acting ability, the evening continued without a hitch.

Although my husband was not awarded the Sailor of the Year for the base, he is the Sailor of a Lifetime to me.

Chapter 29

Empty Nest Syndrome and Ego-Driven Choices

The years flew by, and our lives were filled with military functions, kids' sporting events, and gatherings with friends and family. My up-and-down appetite issues continued.

During these years, I began experiencing pain that would stop me in my tracks. Pain that I can only describe as feeling like something was inside of me, twisting and turning my bowel. I believe that if I had gone to a doctor, I would have been diagnosed with irritable bowel syndrome. I did not see a doctor, but I did start eating yogurt.

I was not prepared for the empty nest to begin when I was only 43 years old! Having had our children one after the other meant that they would move on one after the other. You don't think about that while in the throes of raising them.

I have read that someone said that the days drag on as

the years fly by. Truer words have never been spoken. Our oldest son had moved away to college some 800 miles away. Our middle was working, getting together with friends, and was very active in his church. He was not home much. Our daughter began college two hours away.

After spending his entire naval career at the same naval base, my husband would be given his final set of orders to a duty station about 600 miles away. Before that move was to take place, however, he was underway on his final 6-month deployment. Having email for the first time was a huge plus, but I was alone in a fairly large 4-bedroom home most of the time. I was incredibly lonely, which lent itself, once again, to a suppressed appetite.

With no need for meal preparations and an upcoming high school reunion, I determined this to be a great time to lose the unwanted weight I had gained after having a hysterectomy a couple of years prior.

My daily routine consisted of coffee and a piece of fruit for breakfast, possibly a salad for lunch or no lunch at all, and a microwaved low-calorie meal for dinner. I spent 30 minutes each evening on the treadmill. I was working part-time, so that helped the time pass. The loneliness, however, was with me each and every day.

In all honesty, though, my ego fueled the weight loss in a way that it had not done before.

I would be going to my 25-year high school reunion weighing less than I weighed at graduation. Yay me! The weekend of the reunion was met with one of the biggest ice storms the area had seen. Power was out all over the city. Although the reunion had not been canceled, most of my classmates chose not to attend, and my husband did not want me driving into that.

Once the terrible disappointment wore off, I was actually able to see clearly how God used it to show me my sin of ego. God will use everything in our lives to reveal the motives of our hearts. I saw how my ego was wrapped up in losing weight so that others would be impressed with my outward appearance.

Again, He had convicted me without condemning me so that I could confess my impure motives and turn from them.

"Therefore, there is now no condemnation for those who are in Christ Jesus." *(Romans 8:1)*

Very soon afterward, I traveled to our daughter's school for her field hockey game. Years later, when I looked at a picture of the two of us, I was shocked at how terribly thin I was. I'm not sure that any of my former classmates would have been impressed after all.

Chapter 30

Empty Nest on Steroids

After our move to his final duty station, I fell into a deep depression. I was miserable being so far away from our kids, especially my daughter. She had been my sidekick all along. We did everything together. We went grocery shopping together every two weeks. I would drive while she clipped coupons. We cleaned the house together, cooked almost every dinner together, and she even worked with me before leaving for college.

I worked mostly part-time for 20 years. I spent most of my days putting piles of information into our database. I would sit there, working on autopilot, and daydreaming about what else I could be doing. It was not a bad place to work; I was just restless, and my creative side, which I didn't even know I had, needed to be fed.

In all my years there, there was a brief period when I was

my happiest. My daughter was hired there for the summer. We had so much fun working together. We came up with a fun scheme and invited two of the men who worked there to join us. They were both great sports and liked to have fun too. The next day, my daughter and I showed up in the same outfit, blue shirts and khaki slacks. We told the folks at work that by the time she came downstairs, there was no time to change. Soon after, the two men walked in wearing the same color combination. Somehow, we convinced our co-workers that it was purely a coincidence.

It was silly and fun, and it brought a bit of laughter to the daily humdrum. My daughter still says to this day that she loved working with me. Since I was part-time and she was full-time, there were days that she would go in without me. She says that she was always so sad when I didn't come too.

Shortly after we moved to our new duty station, our oldest son reconnected with a lovely young woman, and they were married soon after. It certainly helped my mood to have them there, but I still struggled with deep sadness. We lived there for two years before returning to the place we had called home for 20+ years.

Our son and his wife moved back to the area at the same time, and I was exactly where I wanted to be: close to my kids again. Once again, with my improving spirits, my weight began to go up more quickly than ever before. While living away for those two years, our second son also met a lovely young woman, and they were married a few months after our return. Two years later, our daughter married her college sweetheart (the one who grew up near the park we visited those many years ago).

From the time of her brothers' weddings until the few months leading up to hers, I had gained more weight than ever before and, once again, went into starvation mode. I wanted her to be proud of me. Clearly, this did not come from her; this was me falling right back into the ego trap that I had sought and received forgiveness for a few short years ago.

It is truly remarkable how God does not give up on us. He stays right with us. He does not become frustrated with us. He already knew on the day that I sought His forgiveness that I would do so again. Unlike ourselves, His patience with us is unlimited. God alone knows our hearts. Often, we do not even know our own. I believe that because God understands us and loves us so deeply, He reveals truth to us as we can grasp it. He uses all of our struggles to end our trying to see His faithfulness toward us. It is a lifetime walk, and He is with us each step of the way.

On the day of my daughter's wedding, I weighed 140 pounds and looked healthy, happy, and not the least bit overweight, even though my weight loss was anything but healthy. She and her husband had considered the advantages and disadvantages of residing in the US or Canada. Canada won out when he was able to get work there after a long search in the US yielded no feasible options.

The day we came home after the wedding, I immediately started down another path of depression and emotional distress. Instead of sleeping the 12-hour drive, I cried the entire drive home. My heart was breaking. I was grieving the loss of what would never be. All her life, I imagined her married with a couple of children and living around the corner. In time, I knew that I absolutely must let all that go to keep our relationship intact with no bitterness or self-pity.

God most certainly answered my prayer, but I spent much time sitting before Him and telling Him all the thoughts and feelings that I could not, would not, tell her. All is well now in my heart and in my spirit, and our relationship has not skipped a beat.

In fact, I have come to understand and accept that she is exactly where she is supposed to be. I do miss her, though. One thing that most certainly helped me get through that time was the birth of our first two grandchildren. This is the role that I believe I was created for.

Just a couple of years after her move to Canada, our middle son and his family moved out of state. Again, my heart was broken. I had become very attached to my granddaughters and had never imagined that they would not be living where we were. After much grief and soul-searching, I came to understand that they were also exactly where they were supposed to be.

Thankfully, we can visit all the families often and for extended visits.

Chapter 31
Doing the Right Thing

I started a journal for each of my grandchildren shortly after they were born. In it, I wrote the words to the songs that I made up and the nicknames I gave to each. I included some photos and my expressions of love for them. Sadly, I did not keep them up. One day, I will give each of them what I have written.

When our 9th and youngest grandchild was two years old, his daddy and sisters, ages seven and nine, moved in with us. Our son was disabled with a degenerative disc disease and had hip replacement surgery soon after moving in. Our small 3-bedroom condo was the perfect size for my husband and me, not so much for three adults and three children.

I had one of the two extra bedrooms set up as my sewing room for the small family business I was working on. We set the other bedroom up for the two girls. Our son was not able to get up and down stairs. He slept on a mattress on the floor in our small living area. The little guy, who has special needs, slept on the couch next to his daddy. This sleeping arrangement continued for several years.

If we knew beforehand exactly what challenges we would face, we would (at least I know I would) do everything in our power to avoid them. I am thankful I did not know or attempt to prevent what God used mightily in our lives.

We were packed in and surrounded by clutter. I had no idea how to fix any of it. Eventually, I moved my sewing area to the other side of the living area, which was designated as a small dining area. Our son and grandson moved into the bedroom where the sewing room had been.

That change alone did much to help my anxiety, but I was still stressed and unhappy most of the time. For the sake of the grandchildren, though, I did my best to keep it to myself. Not an easy task and not a healthy decision (again!) Every once in a while I considered seeking council, but even the thought of that made me anxious.

Where would I even begin?

My mind is a muddled mess.

I am a terrible grandmother.

Why can't I keep our home the way I did when raising my children?

I must make my little business successful so that we can better provide.

Despite all the reasons to do so, I decided that seeking council was just adding one more thing to my plate. I passed on the idea.

I am truly thankful that the three grandchildren have been

in the care of a licensed counselor since their world was turned upside down. Much like the difficult military deployment that had no expiration date, neither did our living situation.

I cannot even put into words all that God worked in my heart during the ten years that we lived together. God will allow exactly what is necessary to work in our hearts when we sincerely ask Him to do so.

I cannot praise Him enough for His grace and mercy, not only for keeping our family together; but also for using the difficult living conditions to teach us the things that truly matter—the things of eternal value.

"Let us not become weary in doing good, for at the proper time we will reap a harvest if we do not give up." (Gal. 6:9)

For me personally, I pray that as I go forward in this life, I will not be so slow to listen.

I will draw on the wonderful truths God has revealed to me. That I will rest in Him.

Trust in Him. Stay very close to Him.

God graciously brought a precious young woman into our son's life, and they were married this past summer. She is so special that I suspect (and I've told her as much) that she is part angel. That is my estimation of her, anyway.

Before this, though, I had started the small business I had alluded to earlier.

Chapter 32

a.j.jacks

The year that the 8th of our nine grands was born, I started my own (very) small business. I wanted the name to be who I am. I wanted it to be my heart. I am, my heart is, quite simply, my family.

My daughter and daughter-in-law were a big part of the business. My daughter-in-law found a pattern-making company that offered a way to use their patterns and sell the clothing that is made. Through a licensing label sewn into each item, we could make and sell as many as we pleased.

The three of us went into high gear. My daughter came down, my daughter-in-law came up, and we worked our own assembly line. I have pictures of sitting at the sewing machine with dresses piled up on every chair around the table.

I had been asking God to help with the name. One night before falling asleep, I thought of all the grands' first names. Then, in my mind, I started arranging and rearranging the first initial of each name, hoping to find something that I liked.

Eventually, I came up with *a.j.jacks*, the first initial of the first seven and the name of the baby born in the year of the start-up. I knew immediately that that was who I was, who we were.

My clothing labels consisted of a logo including *a.j.jacks* and my byline "because gramma says sew." After the name had been established, an unexpected new baby entered our family. Once again, I was wracking my brain to include our newest little. After much thought, I added a division under a.j.jacks and named it *5th generation color works,* as the new baby was named after his daddy, grampa, and great grandpa, making him a 5th generation namesake. That name would be found on items involving paper, such as the few greeting cards we made and our business cards.

We did quite a few craft fairs, and I sold a few things through children's shops. I gave it all I had, but alas, the day came when a difficult decision had to be made. We were spending a whole lot more than we were bringing in; thus, my darling a.j.jacks had to close. Within a short time, I learned that the label program was no longer available.

Many years later, I opened it back up with a completely different inventory. I was now working on my own; my girls were busy raising their families, and their days were full. My focus was on making handmade home decor and fashion.

Once again, I was on the craft fair circuit. If I thought I'd not done well with children's clothing, this was a total bust. Not because the items I made were inferior. In fact, I had customers rave over my rugs and other items. I had more than one fellow vendor tell me that my work was better suited for a more upscale market. But the simple fact is, no matter how hard I tried to find that market, I never did.

One might think that I would be depressed and defeated. But I am not. I have wonderful memories of it all. When my business was all about children's clothing, I had five of the cutest little models. The photos of all my little ones dressed in mix-and-match outfits are priceless. I do not have any regrets about starting or ending my business.

A life lived fully will be full of lessons. Lessons learned to bring growth and wisdom, and peace. I spent those years doing something I loved. I still love sewing. I also much prefer giving to trying to sell. I enjoy sewing more than ever now. At some point during the business building years, though, my intestinal issues flared like never before.

Chapter 33

Gastro Escalation!

Those years of being with my kids and grandkids so often were my happiest. Even though most of us lived far apart, we were incredibly blessed (and still are) to see them often. The ten years of living with three of them built an extraordinary bond.

Because we were able to stay in the others' homes for extended periods of time, we truly got to know them. We built strong bonds with each of them and attended many parties and activities with them.

I got to know each one closely so I could bond with them about the things that mattered to them. It is a bit more difficult to do so when they get older, but it is still possible. You just have to work at it.

The weight gain that had been synonymous with contentment and happiness was evident once again. Contentment and happiness are certainly synonymous with grandchildren for me.

As the pounds piled on, I made the decision to lose weight

in what I considered to be the healthy way. I joined a clinic whose plan included B6 shots in the belly to boost metabolism and meals that consisted of almost nothing but raw fruits and vegetables.

Several weeks after starting the program, I had bunion surgery and ended up in the emergency room after a fall from the crutches. That would be the last time I ever used crutches. I basically have no balance.

I was given a powerful pain narcotic at a local ER and sent home. After a restless night of acid reflux, nausea, and pain, I awoke very sick. After a couple of days and getting sicker, my husband took me to the naval hospital emergency room, where a nurse asked if she could accompany me to the bathroom.

The ER was very busy, and even though there were no beds available, she decided after evaluating my situation that I needed to be taken right in. I was actually put in a closet.

Interestingly, this was not the first time this had happened, but under very different circumstances.

I was taken back to 1976 when I was pregnant with our second son. A sister-in-law who had recently given birth raved about her doctor and was sure I would too. By the time I figured out that he was not a good fit for me, I found that I did not have the gumption to say anything.

Fast forward to the day of birth. Throughout the pregnancy, I did have the gumption to remain adamant about having a natural birth. He did not like this at all. I later figured out that the reason this doctor was ideal for my sister-in-law was that she was comfortable with him making all the decisions. That worked well for her, but it was not for me.

I had not been in the hospital very long before my labor was well underway. Around 4:00 p.m., the doctor stood at the end of my bed, looking disgruntled as I was completely focused on my labor. He decided that since it would be quite some time before the baby was born, he would go to dinner.

At 4:30, my baby was arriving. The nurse started pushing my bed toward the delivery room while simultaneously trying to push the baby back in. In a panic, she wheeled me into a closet, grabbed a passing intern, and insisted that he deliver the baby. He did. After checking my baby out and giving him to me, he left. Then the nurse left also.

My husband, baby, and I remained in that closet for at least an hour before anyone came to take my little guy to the nursery. We bonded beautifully, but it was surely strange.

Birthing stories always fascinate me—even my own.

Back to my current closet stay. As I said, this closet stay was for a very different reason. A portable toilet was placed between my bed and some buckets and mops in the cramped utility closet. My husband had just enough space to sit beside the bed.

I was the sickest I had ever been. In case I died, I made sure to tell my husband how much I loved him. I truly felt that I might die. It seems overly dramatic now, but it was exactly how I felt that day.

In time, I was taken to a room. Because my foot was still bandaged up, and I could not put any weight on it from the bunion surgery, I was unable to use the bathroom in the room.

Another portable toilet was set up beside the bed. Getting in and out of bed with a bandaged and throbbing foot was daunting. I did this all that day, all night, and into the following day. All while being evaluated by one doctor after another. Because the military hospital is a teaching hospital, I was visited by every doctor and intern in the ward. I was later taken for a colonoscopy.

The night before, a very handsome and kind young doctor had brought in two 1-gallon bottles of prep that I was to drink. I was so weak and so nauseous that my expression must have spoken louder than my pitiful words. I looked at him and said that I would try. He looked at me with the kindest expression, picked up the bottles, and said, "Never mind, I'm not going to make you do this!"

I loved that doctor.

The head of the gastrointestinal unit performed my colonoscopy. He described my colon as looking like a red Ferrari! Later, when I relayed this to my daughter-in-law, she commented, "As opposed to a pink Cadillac?"

"Why yes, actually!" I replied after a good laugh.

I was diagnosed with ischemic colitis. There was no definitive cause that the doctors could determine. I knew, however, that it might have had something to do with the powerful narcotic. I absolutely believe to this day that it had everything to do with the raw fruits and veggies diet I had been on.

My system, which had been fragile for years, could not digest so many raw foods.

Alas, it would be the last time I dieted. While I am still

overweight, I am not dieting and will never diet again. My weight is going down gradually by adding some fermented drinks and foods and eating most other foods in moderation. I get pangs from time to time that are much less intense than those caused by ischemic colitis. They warn me to recap what I've been eating and make changes accordingly.

Just recently, I had an ankle replacement surgery. The three-day hospital stay included powerful pain meds and the same at home. After five days of severe gastric discomfort, I stopped the narcotics and started taking acetaminophen, only to find out that it had the same effect.

Dealing with surgical pain without powerful meds is not pleasant, but neither is the gastrointestinal issues that come with it for some folks like me.

I am just now coming to terms with the damage caused by years of poor choices in regard to my overall well-being. It has taken me almost 50 years to put all the pieces of the puzzle together to get to the truth. Years of yo-yo dieting, stress and anxiety wreaking havoc, and an obsession with my outward appearance were recipes for complete and utter failure.

Learning to apply God's word to our everyday lives is instrumental in maintaining a balanced mind, body, and spirit. I share my weight and digestive journey with others to discourage diets or losing weight for the sake of outward appearance. It is a slippery slope down a mountain that is costly to attain and impossible to remain upon.

I am incredibly grateful that my daughter did not go down that self-destructive path despite the fact that I truly was her most important role model. Perhaps, by the grace of God, she was able to do as I said and not as I did.

I am equally grateful that my five granddaughters are being raised by women who understand the importance of a healthy body image. Their most important role models are saying, "Do as I say AND do as I do." My precious granddaughters are listening and following.

I have learned the hard way that mental and physical wellness, as well as body image are far too important to ignore. I pray that women may be wise and love and encourage each other and ourselves in a healthy manner.

Most especially, I pray that we pass our wisdom on to the generations that follow and embrace this absolute truth, ". . . I am fearfully and wonderfully made . . . " (*Psalm 139:14*)

Chapter 34

Did I Mention I Was a Habitual Liar?

was! It was as natural for me to lie as it was to walk. I am no longer, thankfully. I don't know the exact moment when I decided to stop taking myself so seriously. I can't remember the first time I laughed at myself. I do know that I would have saved myself from agony and unnecessary embarrassment due to the stronghold of ego if I had done so long before I did.

God had a lot to work on in me, and these things take time. Being freed from self-mindednesss is truly liberating.

It is exhausting trying to be something or someone that we were never created to be nor can be. Perfection is an unachievable goal. We are created perfectly imperfect. No one is created to walk through this life like a robot, programmed to always perform only at the highest levels. I believe we all know that deep inside. Why, oh why, then, do we hold others and ourselves to such high standards?

I always marveled at people who seemed to be so very comfortable in their own skin. I wanted to be like that too. But how could I be someone I was not? Ah! How could I be someone I was not? Isn't that exactly what I'd done most of my childhood and adulthood?

No wonder I was not comfortable in my own skin; I didn't even know who the real me was. Somehow, sometime in my childhood, I began to conform to whatever I thought I was supposed to be, based on my perception of what was expected.

My go-to coverup for any mess-ups along the way was to lie. I would lie to cover my tracks. I would lie to make myself look good. I would lie to please others. I would lie to cover up a lie. It was habitual, and it was easy. I most certainly would lie to get what I wanted, particularly in my teens. It came so naturally to me, and rarely did I ever get caught or called out for it.

What does habitually lying have to do with learning to take myself less seriously?

Everything! Every time I lied, I was pretending to be something or someone I was not. So, I was habitually being someone I was not. I was being someone I thought I should be, who I thought others wanted me to be. I was habitually manipulating to get what I wanted. I will say that I did not lie with the purpose of hurting others. It was purely my own self-preservation or selfishness.

How and why did this develop in me at such a young age? It is a question I may never know the answer to. It remains a mystery, but it also has been addressed by my loving Father with the same grace and mercy He has always shown me.

When I became a Christian, I didn't realize that much of what I was doing was not God's will for me. Being a Christian is a life-long process of unlearning and learning anew. When we are first saved, we do not automatically become perfect. We do not automatically stop sinning. In fact, the closer we come in our relationship with God, the more aware we become of sin.

But God does begin to show us the areas of our lives that are to be a part of our past. After my conversion, God began to speak to my spirit concerning lying. He did so over a silly lie, but nonetheless, a lie. Lying was still very much a part of my make-up.

We had invited my in-laws over one evening, and I had made a cake earlier that day. The truth is I had made two cakes, but I was embarrassed that the first one didn't turn out. It was not pleasing to the eye. My pride was at stake. I had married into a family of amazing cooks, and my mother-in-law was the epitome of amazing in the kitchen. I left the imperfect cake in the pan on top of the refrigerator for later.

The evening went well, and the second cake looked perfect and was delicious. As I was in the kitchen cleaning, my mother-in-law came in and spotted the cake on top of the fridge. Of course, she was curious about it. I gave a vague answer as to why it was there, but my answer had nothing to do with the truth. She accepted my explanation with no further questions.

As soon as they left, I began feeling bad about lying. The

Holy Spirit was convicting me. I called her later and explained everything to her. She was gracious, understanding, and encouraging. I knew that God allowed her to see the cake and comment in order to speak to my heart through His Holy Spirit.

When we respond in obedience, He so very kindly points out our sin in love. My days of habitually lying were behind me!

Chapter 35

Free Indeed

As I stated, I am not sure of the exact moment when I stopped taking myself so seriously, but I do know that it coincided with a life-changing revelation. I discovered a completely new way of seeing everything. It was new to me but certainly not hidden.

More accurately, the root of this obsessive need to be someone I was not or someone I thought I should be was revealed *to* me rather than discovered *by* me. My over-emphasized self-awareness was a recipe for unhappiness. We can never find peace and joy and true happiness as long as everything in our lives is seen through our own lens.

As I sought God for truth, I found myself asking Him to set me free from self-mindedness and instead cause me to be others-minded. Focusing on the needs of others, listening to others, seeing others, and loving others is so incredibly liberating. In true Godly fashion, He has given more than I even asked by giving me the gift of laughing at myself.

Instead of feeling like an idiot and making a scene over my epic bowling fail, I was able to laugh at myself. Even more, it gave me such great pleasure to imagine how funny it was for the group of ten-year-old boys to witness the old lady sliding halfway down the lane with her fingers still inside the bowling ball. Instead of getting upset and feeling foolish when I slipped and fell hard onto my buttocks from an onion on the grocery store floor, I was able to laugh right along with my niece, imagining what she witnessed.

These are two of many instances that had far different outcomes since I had been set free from taking myself too seriously.

"So if the Son sets you free, you will be free indeed." *(John 8:36)*

Thank you, God, that as long as I am still breathing, You will complete the good work You have begun, and You will continue to set me free. I look forward, with great anticipation, to His continued work in the areas of my life that need His deliverance. I know He will faithfully do so as I seek Him, wait upon Him, and rest in Him.

". . . he who began a good work in you will carry it on to completion until the day of Christ Jesus." *(Phil. 1:6)*

Chapter 36

Embracing Hope

My middle name is Hope. My nickname since birth is Sandy. I learned at an early age that I was named, in part, after my aunt, the youngest of my mother's eight surviving siblings. All six of her brothers served in World War 2. All but one returned alive.

When I was a toddler, I was asked to be a flower girl at my namesake's wedding. I know this not from memory but because my mother mentioned it often when I was growing up. It always made me a little sad that it didn't work out. I would love to have photos from such a special occasion.

But it was not to be, and I am pretty sure that had everything to do with the fact that my dad worked overnight hours for the B & O Railroad and was not able to make the just over 100-mile trip for the rehearsal. My mother did not drive. It is interesting that my aunt always was, and still is, my favorite of the five aunts on both sides of my family. I suppose I felt a special connection to her since she wanted me to be a part of her big day.

Even if that were not the case, I was drawn to her. She is one of the coolest, funnest (even if that weren't a word, I would still use it), kindest, most loving, and lovable folks to grace this earth. We spent a lot of time with her and her family when we were young. I really can't say enough about her, and I am proud to share the same middle name with such an amazing woman.

That was not always the case. I never told her this, nor did I ever mention it to my parents. Because I was so self-conscious, I was embarrassed by anything that brought attention to me. In my mind, a name like Hope would bring much unwanted attention. Where or why that thought took root, I have no idea. Except that this was true of so many things for me as a child.

From time to time, someone would find out, and I would be mortified. I remember exactly how I felt in the pit of my stomach and exactly how it felt when an internal heat began to turn my face bright red. A boy on our elementary school bus started calling me 'Hopey.' He was laughing and yelling loud enough for everyone to hear. Of course, all the kids joined in on the taunt. It's what kids do.

My face burned, my eyes filled, and my sobs were heard by all. I never knew who told him my closely guarded secret, but I do know that he very soon regretted his decision to use it against me. My older sister laid into him and took him down. He was a big kid, but size was never an issue once she was provoked. Nothing provoked her more than someone picking on her sister, who was three years her junior. He never did that again, and he may or may not have needed a Band-Aid or three for his face. You see, while I was a nail biter, my sister was notorious for her long nails and her willingness to use them. She used them against me plenty of times, but as with most families, nobody else better hurt my sibling.

Eventually, he and I became very good friends all the way through high school. We are even friends on Facebook. I wonder if he even remembers any of this.

When we were teens, my sister and I were walking, out in the country where we lived, with a girl we had just met. We were chatting away, getting to know each other, and for reasons I do not remember, we were telling each other our middle names.

My sister, who was named after one of our grandmothers, shared hers. I looked at our new friend, and she at me, but neither of us wanted to spill the beans. Each of us was certain that hers was surely much worse than the others.

We decided to count to three and say our names at the same time. We each kept our word and blurted out 'Hope' at the exact same time. We were shocked! We had a great laugh and quickly moved on to other subjects. I would never know why she felt the same about the name as I did.

Strangely, I had never seen her before or after that day. I have no recollection of her first or last name. But to this day, I remember her as 'the other Hope.'

Not long after that, I began to share my middle name more openly. In fact, a group of seven of us who had lunch together decided to start a club. We came up with a name for our club using some of our middle names and some of our nicknames. Guess who was not the least embarrassed or upset when her name was the first of the seven? Hopey!

We had a great time with our exclusive lunch club. It was silly. The group spent a lot of time together in and out of school. My middle name would never be a cause for embarrassment again, but it would be several years before I embraced it as who I am.

When I became a Christian at 21 years of age, changes slowly began in my heart. For the past 49 years, I have learned many things about myself and God. The more I learn about God, the more I realize that I have yet to learn. It truly is a life-long journey of faith. Over the years, I have grown in self-esteem.

Ironically, or perhaps not, the less attention we pay to ourselves, our own wants, and our own comforts, the more others-minded we become and the more our self-esteem finds its rightful place in our lives.

It happens in baby steps for some like myself. Over time, the various trials and difficult situations that were out of my control have filled me with much hope, not in myself but in my God, who never disappoints.

"Therefore, since we have been justified through faith, we have peace with God through our Lord Jesus Christ, through whom we have gained access by faith into this grace in which we now stand. And we boast in the hope of the glory of God. Not only so, but we also glory in our sufferings because we know that suffering produces perseverance; perseverance, character; and character, hope. And hope does not put us to shame, because God's love has been poured out into our hearts through the Holy Spirit, who has been given to us." (*Romans 5-1-5*)

As we grow in faith through the various trials, these words speak to our hearts in a way that we can truly understand and in a way that we cannot quite grasp without having experienced such trials.

As I came to understand this, I came to realize that Hope is who I am!

I am full of Hope! When I say the word "hope," I have what seems to be an actual positive vibe run through me from deep within that I simply cannot explain with mere words.

My desire in this, all too often seemingly hopeless world is that those I connect with will sense the hope within me and understand that this same hope is available to them.

For this reason, this memoir, as well as everything I write, is done so under the name that defines me, the name that I embrace, Sandy Hope.

All scripture is from the New International Version Bible.

My baby photo. Clearly thriving
on whole cow's milk

Me as a shy second grader

Our wedding day, October 21, 1972

Memphis, TN, I was pregnant with #3

My boys and my girl. Ages 3, 16 months and newborn.

One of our many trips to the Memphis zoo.
The kids and grands still kid Bill about his short-shorts.

My sisterfriend who was with me when my daughter was born.
She is my sister-in-law but we don't use the in-law part.
We have been together through thick and thin!

Helicopters like the ones used in the Iranian Hostage
Rescue Attempt Mission

Our family shortly after the failed mission 1980

The converted Charley-O Van and our camper. The six kids slept in
the van and the four adults, in the camper. We packed and unpacked
every single day, in search of the elusive 'perfect' campsite.
In reality, they all were.

Six little munchkins all in a row for breakfast.
We had no idea then that the little one on the far left would be
marrying a fella who lived not too far from there.

Niagara Falls

Running from some pesky Canadian mosquitoes

A get-together with my two high school besties 1990's

I had the cutest little models for my short-lived
a.j.jacks clothing line.

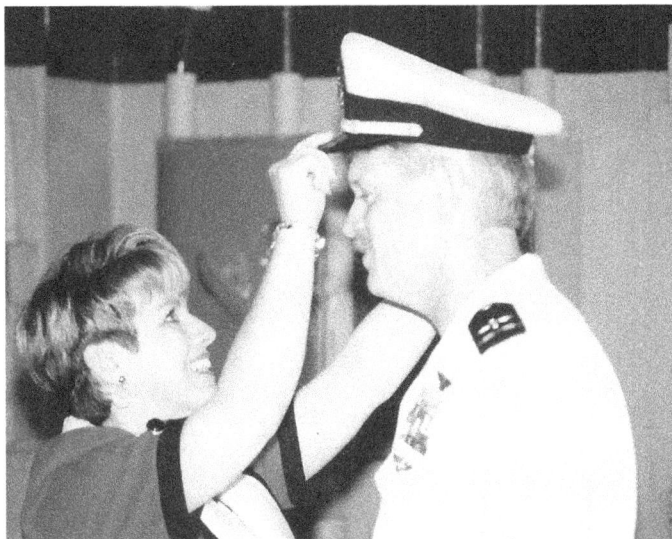

Placing the hat on my newly commissioned
Naval Chief Warrant Officer 1994

Celebrating our 50th Wedding Anniversary on a cruise.

Acknowledgments

I would venture to say that few, if any, who write a book would be able to boast that it was done with no help from others. I am no acceptation to this.

The only down side to recognizing those who have been instrumental in making my memoir an actual book, is that I am sure to miss someone. It is inevitable because it would seem that almost everyone in my life has played a part in my story.

That being said, I will attempt to give my whole-hearted thanks to these few. Thank you, dear husband of mine! Your patience and calm demeanor made you the perfect mate for this girl and my all-over-the-place emotions, especially in the early years. What a blessing it is to have come through so much in our 50+ years together. I hope and pray we have many more "Good Morning" greetings followed by many more "Good Nights" for years to come. I love you most!

Thank you, my darling children, for your encouragement and support from the moment I mentioned writing my memoir. I adore you all!

Thank you, precious friends (some of you are family as well) for giving me the incredible blessing of your life-long friendships.

And to my grandchildren, thank you for loving me so well. You inspire me to love the Lord more each and every day, to be better and to do better. I need only think of you to be reminded of God's great love for me.

Ava • Savanna • Cecelia • Aidan • Jacqueline • Jordan Kirsten • Jack • Liam—You Are My Heart.